The freedom of the mind is also freedom for the body.

The two are synonymous.

TIME'S UP

Shining A Light On Darkness

Aletheia Rose

To order additional copies of this book, contact:
Xlibris
800-056-3182
www.Xlibrispublishing.co.uk
Orders@Xlibrispublishing.co.uk
774760

Contents

ACKNOWLEDGEMENTS

It is a pleasure to thank all those who have helped me with my book.

I would like to thank all those wonderful people who help survivors and the unsung heroes who tirelessly help those who have been raped or beaten and need shelter.

Thanks to Kathrin Herr from the Writing Mechanic for helping me with the entire editorial work, which immensely helped; Tim Tarango, from California, for the amazing support and training in the NLP training course and advice; and Dexter from Xlibris for all the support.

Blessings to the Online Church in San Antonio, USA, and Daren Wood in the UK for speaking truth and words of encouragement—such great pastoral guidance.

I would like to thank Andy H. for his integrity and observations, Nigel Ward for the investigative material (the eyes and ears in north UK, with some reference material), and Mike Clarke for his references.

Thanks for the photography: Sun-coast Weddings in Florida and MJ Photography for the covers and my crown photo inside.

Thanks to Life Changers: Kerri Parker Academy, and the sponsors for awarding me the Classic Model of the Year UK (2017)—my first ever beauty queen crown.

Also, thanks to Miss Diamond for awarding me Classic Diamond Photogenic 2018 and also Chloe Avon for taking me on as a professional model, for including me in Guinness World Records 2018, for awarding me Miss Severn Diamond Glamorous UK, and for her relentless charity work for the homeless through Red Bag Co.

I would like to thank all my readers for reading my book, and I wish you all peace.

I dedicate this book to all the victims who have endured abuse. Let you beauty shine. We are all beautiful. Don't let any person dim your light.

Do you bring in a lamp to put it under a bowl or a bed? Instead, don't you put it on a stand? For whatever is hidden is meant to be disclosed, and whatever is concealed is meant to be brought out into the open.

Mark 4:21

Introduction

I wrote this book to enable readers to identify and recognize abuse and the trauma it can potentially create. I also want you, my readers, to have second-hand knowledge of my survival so that you might relate to me and find relief in knowing that you're not alone. I want to speak about what is considered taboo, and I seek to support you in your own healing process.

The freedom of the mind is also freedom for the body. The two freedoms are synonymous. Within the chapters, I cover many different kinds of abuses, and the impact which can potentially last for many years. In the later part of the book there are different sources of information to help with recovery. I have included parts of my journal and my breakthroughs to support the reader. Many survivors and allies have had their healing thwarted by their lack of access to knowledge and therapy techniques. This book is also meant to impart knowledge and inspire survivors by empowering them. I have corresponded with and trained alongside many persons who have witnessed abuse.

The emotional overload from traumatic experiences can leave a person feeling helpless, and energy levels can remain low due to the constant stress hormone. Abuse can shatter a sense of security, and a person can feel their life or well-being continually threatened by assimilating current situations to previous events or past abuses.

Perpetrators manipulate their victims and can use any method to gain control of their victim—like they are a possession. Victims and survivors are not responsible for the behaviors of the abusers. Even though abusers make their victims/survivors feel like it's their fault, it is not.

Abusers can even make victims doubt their own thoughts, and quash their self-esteem or confidence. Poisonous thoughts can lead to limiting beliefs or self-blame which can prevent a person from reaching his or her goals and obliterate any drive.

Unfortunately, perpetrators often try to get the victims alone and make them feel special or build an intimate relationship with them, as in the Boko Haram girls who were abducted in Africa. Stockholm syndrome can develop; the emotional attachment towards their perpetrator allows abusive situations to continue due to the bond they have created with their abusers, often for victims own survival. Also, people with less social mobility become lonely and susceptible to a Stockholm syndrome relationship or can be easily taken advantage of.

This book is meant to confront all forms of abuse, to define it and describe it so as to remove the stigma towards it in public conversation, and to allow victims of abuse to recognize it and seek help and healing.

Healing is a journey and can be uncomfortable at times. As you become more aware of certain behaviors, you will gain more power to make any necessary changes in order to have harmonious relationships and spot abusive traits. It's so rewarding when you break through previous traumas and reach beyond what was your previous limitation and gain a sense of accomplishment that the worst is over and the best is yet to come. We no longer need to be numb to our feelings. We can obtain healing by freeing up those stored emotions. Let this book be a light on your journey towards healing.

CHAPTER 1

What Is Abuse?

As we begin on our discussion of abuse and healing, let's first define abuse so we can learn to recognize it.

Abuse is an illegal or improper action towards another person. Abuse can be used to gain an unfair benefit over someone else by many means: finances, verbal, physical strength, exploitation, violence, intimidation, aggression, rape, violations, emotions, age, sex, social sabotage, emotional blackmail, disability, etc.

People who abuse others do so to gain an advantage over them, or benefit from the other person who is in a lesser position. The abusers can project their self-imposed superiority on to their victims to feed their own egos. Many people don't question behavior but are taught to imitate those around them. That doesn't mean this kind of action is right, especially if it hurts someone else, as that which occurs in dysfunctional families, social conditioning.

Social conditioning behavior starts early in our lives and has permeated through social development. A good leader has a positive benefit and can be challenged without adverse repercussions, but negative or abusive leadership has a detrimental effect, which can create long-term suffering that may not surface for many years.

An abuser can exhibit many emotions. They can use anger; they can ball up their fists to intimidate others or point their finger at others rather than take responsibility over something that has happened. If you challenge an abuser, they may become violent. Precursors can be visual stares, snide remarks, or name-calling which belittles the victim. This behavior often comes after months of charming and overly nice allure. This allure quite often comes as a shock to a victim when the charm turns to personal attacks. A victim will reflect back on the nice captivation they liked initially, and see these new behavior episodes as "out of character", so the victim simply tries to brush it off.

It is very difficult to identify an abusive person, because often they present a very enigmatic character. They can seem genuinely interested and flattering in everything you're doing and make seemingly constructive suggestions. Slowly, signs become apparent. Abusive people may eliminate those whom they consider a threat and start alienating their victims from these threats. Abusers create a situation in which they use their position to control the situation. Child abuse or sexual abuse it becomes more sinister—such as when touching or innuendos start or the abuser starts controlling the situations adversely—that victims may feel a bit awkward and unsure. But because the perpetrator has built up a good rapport, the victim often overlooks these red flags. Many victims are simply not aware they are being 'groomed'. Over time, victims become subconsciously compliant and slowly lose their individual sense of worth, especially if the perpetrator has put comments into the victim's thoughts that they "need" the perpetrator. Then a victim becomes dependent upon the perpetrator.

There's an array of behavior traits that signify an abusive relationship/ person: insulting, subtle jibes, persistently finding faults, or overt insults progressing to embarrassment in public. Humiliation is meant to create submissiveness and to control the victim in front of others. It is meant to push a person to be subservient.

Many times a person actually means no harm and yet the tongue and cheek sarcasm can be perceived as verbally abusive, especially to an observer. Narcissists and sociopaths are potentially dangerous, and they are often master manipulators.

In one case, predator teacher/coach made sexual advances towards a student. When another student complained about the predator's overly sexual behavior towards his friend, the complaining student was ostracized by the predator and peers in the group. The peers were socially conditioned by parameters to conform to the teacher's draconian rules. The peers didn't make a stand because they feared being ridiculed or receiving lower marks, which would affect their future. Meanwhile, the complainant was ostracized by his peers, and his marks were lowered as a form of punishment from the teacher for not falling into the line of authority or hierarchy, and this behavior allowed the predator to manipulate his subjects to conform and get away with his sexual advances. This is manipulation and abuse of a position of authority. This behaviour filters down to many students who continue this abusive and new learnt behaviour amongst peers. Sexual abuse can permeate throughout a campus, and nearly 49% of female students said they were inappropriately touched and only 5% reported it to anyone in authority. This survey by Absolute research was conducted by 5,649 university students, however the office of national statistics 2018 say less than 20% of victims report sexual crime.

In careers that have hierarchical systems, if the person at the helm is particularly corrupt or abusive, workers can experience detrimental effects, especially on their mental health, which can cause more sick days and high turnover of employment. Some employees can manipulate this weakness by blackmail for their own agendas. When employees become complicit to multifaceted abuse, it can create a web of more industrial corruption. This behavior can become normal, and employees often stay quiet and comply in order to receive their pay. Reports of historical abuse cases and violations of human rights have been surfacing, coming from many industries on an industrious scale. Often when the hierarchy falls, victims are left to process their feelings, and eventually, the truth comes out.

Ongoing investigations into these alleged systematic cases have shown the widespread corruption and abuse that stretches across many industries, with several victims that have survived and suffered for many years. Examples include the Operation Hydrant for historical child abuse cases; Operation Fairbank for child abuse cases involving many politicians; Operation Athabasca for the historical child abuse cases related to Elm Guest House; Operation Midland for investigating murders and child abuse by many people in positions of power across the South of England and in Dolphin House Estate; Operation Cayacos; Operation Whistle, which investigated Edward Heath, who was a former British prime minister; Operation Yewtree for cases against Jimmy Savile and others; and Operation Pallial, an inquiry into the care system of North Wales and Scotland.

Other historic child abuse cases have also highlighted human trafficking. Babies were taken from orphanages in the fifties and shipped out to Australia to await a new fate with their adoptive parents. They were quite often being abused. Many children's care homes are involved in historic abuse cases. In Mexico, the head of a church, Father Maciel, was found to have been abusing young boys. When Pope John Paul II heard that the abuse had occurred, he took no action. Father Maciel accompanied him on a papal visit in Mexico on three occasions. The canons lawyer made it clear that their loyalty was to the church and not to Father Maciel's victims.

In 2014, a study commissioned by the Catholic Church found that more than 4,000 priests in the US had faced sexual abuse allegations in the last fifty years, with over 10,000 victims testifying against them. Pedophile cases hit the headlines within the Catholic Church in the USA, Ireland, and Australia. When Pope Benedict XVI became pope, he took action to eradicate the predator priests. In 2011–12, he defrocked 384 priests. He admitted that his predecessor had committed deplorable neglect of his post in not eradicating these abusers.

The church has been in the spotlight for child abuse, which is a prolific issue across many Catholic and Anglican dioceses worldwide. The pope addressed this issue and is bringing in measures to penalise this behaviour and declare it unacceptable. In some countries, the legal penalty has proved to be a deterrent for abusers, but in other countries, the law is somewhat lenient.

A few celebrity and political names have been in the tabloids for the abuse of children and exploitation of young innocent people. A pedophile club, the PIE (Pedophile Information Exchange), had government officials as members (or sponsors); it was founded on 1974 and disbanded in 1984. It was an activist group that campaigned for the abolition of age consent for sex and also had a helpline for members on how to deal with resistant children against sex. A former naval officer was accused of a string of rape and sexual assaults against boys as young as ten. He lured young boys into his home with the promise of meals and a day out, the courts heard. Other members used his bikes to lure young boys. Often, the troubled young boys from broken homes were passed around between the predators to be raped. The defendants used the defence of how homosexuality has changed, but these boys were lured in, and these predators took full advantage of the boys' vulnerabilities, which is clearly sexual abuse. The predator was tracked down and found in the Philippines, where he was abusing scores of young boys before being caught.

Regardless of the kind of abuse, it can be difficult to comprehend why and how someone could victimise you. Sometimes abusers don't even realize what they're doing is wrong, as they have imitated the behaviour of another person or been commanded to do a particular task, often by another in authority. If this behaviour has never been condemned, it creates a pattern where their abusive behaviour becomes a norm to them.

Abusers do not often see their actions as abusive; they cannot accept that it is their behaviour which is wrong, and they continue to abuse or sexually harass or bully others.

This fact leads me to conclude that abuse is a pattern of behaviour that is deeply embedded in some parts of society. The situation has not been addressed, and not enough measures have been implemented to root out abuse and predators. Only a very small portion of abusers go to prison, and quite often it happens years after the abuse occurred, if they haven't already died from old age, before being penalized.

In the UK especially, we have created a society that is wrapped up in bureaucracy and reams of paperwork. The expensive law system is actually a hindrance to victims, and where they are subjected to invasive questioning, which often compounds a trauma. Though there are a few free drop-in help centres in the UK, we have Citizens Advice, whose centres are manned by volunteers who have a law background. There are also a few helpline numbers, which I include below, though the list is not exhaustive.

- In the USA, Family Hope Center (dyslexia, ADHD, autism, etc.): 1-610-397-1737
- In the USA, RAINN (rape helpline): 1-800-656
- In the UK, Salvation Army (homeless helpline): 0300-303-8151
- In the UK, Acas (workers' rights): 0300-123-1100
- In the UK, Survivors UK: 0203-598-3898
- In the UK, Family Lives (bullying helpline): 0808-800-222
- In the UK, Childline: 0800-1111

Though there aren't nearly enough institutional help centers, there are many people and organizations in the UK who want to help victims of abuse. Use the numbers above if you need to, along with the many other resources I will list throughout this book.

Torn Down Time and Time Again

I offer my story as one of hope for survivors to be able to take the first step towards healing and to encourage allies of survivors to never stop standing up for those who have less power and who have been victimized. Together, we can protect all of our basic human rights.

My experience will filter through at the end of each chapter. I will bring awareness to the causes and effects of abuses. I know many of my readers have also experienced similar abuses, or would like to understand more.

Within this book I have brought attention to some of the behaviors I have personally experience, and researched, that are associated with some perilous situations/ abuse. Most people are totally unaware of any abusive traits or red flags until it's too late. Not all red flags lead to physically violent people, or child abusers etc however these traits are more than often associated with the relevant perpetrator. I have broken down each chapter into different forms of abuses, so that you can choose what is relevant, or you can read it all.

After a trauma we often try to blank it out and deny it ever happened but the associated stimuli can still affect us. However the good news is that we can process our thoughts and feelings, which can unblock fears and release obstacles that have held us back over time. We can also process toxic patterns of behavior, to understand and empower ourselves.

I have identified many gaps in the system which doesn't necessarily support every person, even if it's their job to do so. We all must strive to be the best we can be, and support others.

Mental health has always been taboo; however abuse does affect a person's mental health. My mental health was thwarted by child abuse, rape, homelessness or sofa surfing, human trafficking, physical assaults, domestic violence, verbal abuse, and financial abuse. I have suffered from most things you can envisage, but with the grace of God, I have overcome the worst effects of post-traumatic stress disorder. My traumas were not addressed by our medical provisions though.

I want to give a little bit of situational explanation so you might better understand my story in the following chapters.

From seven I was sexually abused by a neighbor, and then at the age of fifteen, I was raped by my friend's father.

Between the ages of fifteen and sixteen, I was homeless or currently known as a sofa surfing, and didn't have much stability, which was a complete contrast to my childhood in which wealth and holidays were the norm. I was very naive, gullible; and totally oblivious to other people's hidden agendas. People did take full advantage of my vulnerable situation many times, and I was almost trafficked to Holland.

I spent a lot of time in total denial as it was all too painful to process; I tried to suppress my unworthy and negative feelings which incidentally seeped into my romantic relationship, where I became co-dependent. A relationship that lasted for several years, but I was being beaten relentlessly and made to feel like I deserved nothing more. I finally decided to leave my abusive boyfriend and took just the basic necessities and moved away to start over. I was safe but being alone was tough. I had it drummed into me that I was worthless and I believed this, I didn't think I deserved anything better. I carried this low self esteem burden for most of my life, so I am hoping you will see my errors and learn: self esteem comes from within and not what others say or do.

At twenty-three years, I took the plunge and took my first qualification, after leaving school with nothing. This vocational qualification was not difficult but the psychological trauma that was associated with walking into an educational environment was so overwhelming. I experienced such intense pain and flashbacks of having to leave school and my friends, that this pain ran very deep.

Time went by, and I was in another romantic relationship, but it wasn't any better. In hindsight, I did not know that my own lack of self-worth and neediness caused me to go after possessive men. I wanted someone to love me, but I was beaten regularly again and controlled not knowing where to turn to, as I suffered from endless physical and emotional pain. I left this yet another abusive relationship after more years of abuse. Now in hindsight, I should have looked at loving myself and pressing into God. I was looking externally for comfort and love.

I decided to move to another location, and another relationship failed, so I started to study and learnt beauty which was my dream job since five years old. The trauma of leaving school at 15 was ignited every time I wanted to learn. I was in my thirties, and I needed to complete those qualifications, or I wouldn't be able to better my prospects or have my dream job. I passed the exams and was offered a managerial role for the season. At the end of that season, I moved into another job vacancy. However it wasn't long before the duty manager started making unwanted sexual advances towards me. I endured verbal threats of being sacked or given less hours if I didn't lie on top of him intimately and do as he said. I became so ill with stress and decided to leave my job, but then I struggled to get the unemployment benefits because I had left my job voluntary.

I had very little money and no job, but I decided to open my own business after this, and luckily, a very Good Samaritan believed in me and helped me financially, giving me a grant to start my business. I had a business for over fifteen years and expanded this a few times.

Finally, I thought I had it all as I reached 40. I got married and had a beautiful wedding. I came back to the UK after the honeymoon and my business rent went up 66%, so I close the bigger business and focused on the mobile business, and my degree. Whilst I was closing the large business I found out I was pregnant and a month later the British law suddenly changed, and I needed to sponsor my husband for him to come from the USA. I had to earn over £18,000 a year, which was impossible, so we looked into USA visas, but that was useless too, so I never saw my husband again. I had my baby in the UK without him, and we divorced five years later because that was the only solution. This was hard for me to come to terms with.

So I plunged myself into my degree, too discovered I was severely dyslexic, and had mild autism; I had totally fallen through the net, but I wasn't surprised at this.

When I was in the middle of my degree my ex partner died and so did Jimmy Saville and the child abuse case came to light, this sent me off on a downward spiral of unwanted feelings and emotions. My mental health was in a bad way, any help fell upon deaf ears, and I became agoraphobic and lived mostly in isolation with my child. I was afraid of everyone and everything, and was diagnosed with PTSD from my past, but there wasn't any support for this, so I embarked on some courses to help me. All my suppressed feelings surfaced quicker that I could comprehend, and I needed to deal with my past traumas.

Healing:

I decided I was going to look at healing myself from all these painful feelings that I was experiencing and to leave no stone unturned. So that was what I did. I had abandonment, money, low self worth, trust issues, self esteem, guilt, shame fear, etc I had traumas from child abuse, and rape etc so it was like opening a can of worms.

I pressed into God, and I knew I had to learn to forgive these abusers no- matter how hard that would be, (not forget) and to forgive myself for holding onto the blame and guilt. I looked into educating myself, to help me move forward with my life, and learn laws, disciplines, exercises, faith etc which can all be found in this book. Sometimes we are dealt a raw hand in life but that doesn't define who we are.

After a year to two of healing, I was able to leave my house, other than to go to clients houses for their beauty. I decided to work part-time for a company to help them; childcare had become an issue, so I prayed that day. Then I went to work, and I was sacked because I couldn't work at weekends (no childcare). Then the same day of losing one job, an acting job came up from out of the blue. I just went with this new direction and I felt like God really had his hand on my life now. The acting was only weekdays, and I was offered the main role. This was awesome but challenging, as it stretched me psychologically having to portrayed different characters for my acting post. I did struggle with some roles in terms of the character as this was so different to who I am. In 2016, my professional acting life was progressing and I was offered a TV comedy series role. Feature film roles followed, along with TV commercials. I have learned so much within this industry, and it's been great fun mostly. I was targeted by sleazy couch directors, but I didn't go to auditions in hotels because something made me feel uneasy to later find out about the widespread abuse.

The acting made me look at psychology from different perspectives, and with the therapies and my faith this pushed me beyond my comfort zone. As I was learning new behaviors I started to look at my limited beliefs. A professor made me question myself and my belief system from a couple of years prior, so I had conflicting thoughts from what he had said- to what others had said previously, so I decided with my to pluck up the courage and enter a beauty pageant. This pageant was a massive personal challenge and tested my belief system and made me push myself out in front of people.

In the first pageant, I didn't even know what to wear. So I tried another, and pressed into God, and with the correct clothes, I won "The Classic Model of the Year UK", I felt so calm and amazed that I had won, and I personally felt I triumphed over those people who put lies into my mind for many years. The lies that made me hideaway, their lies which told me I wasn't good enough, the people who said I looked old and had chicken legs. All those comments had chipped away at me for years and I spent most of my life believing what others had said about me, and when I won I had to gather my thoughts, and I actually felt proud for going out there, in front of a crowd, doing a catwalk and modeling in my late 40s and winning. I found out what it felt like to have self esteem. This was a victorious moment, over my abusers who lied and abused me over the years where I felt worthless. This victory changed my life...this crown was a symbol of this victory; this is what God wanted me to win and to show all the victims and survivors that there is hope, and not to give up.

I dedicate my crown to all the victims and survivors of abuse and to let you to know you are all loved. I knew this wasn't just my moment but a victorious moment for all who had suffered at the hands of abusers.

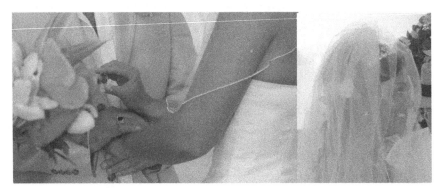

Wedding photo

Me acting

CHAPTER 2

Child and Young Learner Abuse

Child abuse can be physical or sexual in nature; it can also consist of neglect, psychological and/or physical violation, or emotional abuse that can potentially result in mental health issues. Child abuse perpetrators may hang around areas where children tend to be. They often seek out vulnerable single parents or go to areas stricken with poverty. They may offer gifts to gain the friendship and confidence of a naive parent or child. Parents are often quite glad for the help, oblivious to the fact that they are being groomed. Child abuse can leave victims with traumatic scars that can surface in adulthood.

A perpetrator can build up trust slowly and appears to be playful and seems supportive. After a while, they start to use words that can seem out of place or are inappropriate. The signs can be subtle and easy to miss. When the opportunity arises, they take it. It usually happens when they have the child alone, and often a child is compliant as they know the predator as an authority figure or an elder. The predator has control over the child, and sexual abuse can sometimes follow. Child abuse often goes completely unnoticed as parents and children are not educated to look for the signs.

Misconduct and young person abuse is more prevalent than most of us realize, and victims more often than not do not report the abuse until decades after the incident, if at all. This is evident with the police reports on the Jimmy Savile abuse; many people reported their suffering of child abuse many years after it occurred.

Many people are too scared to speak out or are restricted by laws and allegations, until the predators are decease, however former INXS singer allegedly had information regarding a VIP pedophile ring in the UK that was connected to the child rapist Jimmy Saville and high ranking politicians before his death in 1997. Michael Hutchence died by strangulation from fabric/belt to a door knob. Chris Cornell a singer was found dead 18 May 2017 by strangulation from an exercise band around his neck, to the doorknob after a show, the verdict was suicide. It was later exposed that he was working with his best friend Chester Bennington from Linkin Park singer to expose an elite pedophile ring. Chris and his wife had previously set up a foundation to help victims of child abuse. Two months later Chester Bennington was found dead by his housekeeper by a doorknob death July 2017. Each death was ruled suicide by local authorities. Robert steele, a former CIA agent revealed there was no hard evidence to confirm his theory. However he suggests there is a strong correlation between doorknob deaths and pedophilia.

Abuse can leave the victim with a lifetime of mental torment and suffering. Victims often do not know it's wrong at the time of a violation, and can feel pressured into staying silent for fear of retribution from their abusers. Shame, fear and suffering often lasts a lifetime, and a child can grow up having difficulty expressing thoughts and feelings. They often learn to use strategies of diversion or avoidance.

Revisiting the traumatic events or place later in life can increase the tension again, bringing sweat, nausea, elevated heart rate, and hyperawareness. The physical body is just as affected as the person's mental capacities. Lethargy can set in, and the person can go into complete denial that their abuse ever happened. They do this in order to create a feeling of safety. Survivors of abuse can bottle up these emotions for years, but with only a word or smell or something else just as minor, that old memory or perhaps the feeling of not being in control can lead to an overload of mixed, negative, unprocessed emotions.

Here are some examples of child abuse cases:

1. Former students of Margaret MacLennan (headmistress at the Royal School for the Blind) recently reported the abuse after the death of the headmistress. Victims described the ordeals they endured and said the headmistress was evil from head to toe. The victims are now in their sixties.

2. Football clubs hit the headlines in 2017 when a professional footballer came forward to speak about child sexual abuse that occurred within the club. Since then, more than twenty former footballers, trainees, and professionals have made allegations. There are eighty-three suspects and ninety-eight clubs involved in the latest enquiry into child abuse cases within football clubs in the UK.

3. Jimmy Savile is a predator who was known for his celebrity fame within the BBC. He was a prolific paedophile who abused children of all ages. He was connected with children's homes and hospitals and had easy access to his victims. This sexual abuse spanned over a few decades, but it was not reported until after his death when his victims, now adults, came forward with their testimonies of abuse.

4. One particularly public situation involved boys who attended a detention centre. Former police superintendent Gordon Anglesea was convicted at age seventy-nine for sexually abusing teenage boys. Anglesea, who received £375,000 in libel damages from the media that accused him of involvement with paedophiles, used his position and connections with authority to molest boys while running a detention centre in Wrexham in the 1980s. The boys who were convicted of minor petty crimes attended on Saturdays. Anglesea would make the youngsters do sit-ups and squat thrusts naked. The victims, now currently in their forties, said Anglesea ruined their lives. One witness said he was passed around 'like a handbag'. The abuse

the boys experienced caused many of them to self-destruct. They committed further crimes and got involved in drugs and alcoholism.

Anglesea's defence payment was funded by the police. He was found to be connected to notorious North Wales paedophile John Allen, among others, who used children's homes as a cover for abusing children. The victims were trafficked to John Allen via Anglesea. Witnesses said Anglesea was a regular visitor to Bryn Alyn children's home in Wrexham, which was run by John Allen. Allen was convicted in 1995. He was jailed for life in 2014. The spokesman for the NSPCC Wales said, 'Gordon Anglesea is a sexual predator who abused a position of trust and authority.' Gordon Anglesea died in prison on 16 December 2016.

Most child abusers hold positions of power over their victims. They can (generalizing) be a form of instructor or a public figure with power, money, and prestige. Every person who works within a school setting are trained to protect children from harm and to spot signs of bullying and abuse. This is easier said than done. A teacher's workload consists of so much, and attempting to watch for signs of abuse may be more than they can handle. It is the duty of caretakers to protect all children in their care, but this clearly hasn't been the case in the past. Many have been complicit to organized abuse. Many schools have fostered safeguarding, but within corrupt organizations, these efforts are not foolproof. Parents and members need to be observant and keep communications open with learners and children. It is our responsibility to make sure vulnerable people are in a safe environment.

Recently, it was discovered that some younger teachers who never had a record were involved in cases of pedophilia. They had no history of abuse, and they passed their disclosure checks. Investigations were also recently launched into claims made by three disabled children who were allegedly abused in a primary school. The children were subjected to physical and emotional abuse. The children's parents stated that they felt the safeguarding that is currently in place at that school does more to protect the teachers than the children.

Most state schools have strict rules for safeguarding, but it has been revealed that boarding schools are potentially an open book for abuse. The statistics (as reported by Nigel Ward from The Examiner) do not have any say in how private schools are run, and a lot of abuse has gone unnoticed due to the limiting safety checks on private institutions. The truth does not come to light until much later because the institutions hide it so well. Many schools have recently been investigated in a pedophile ring, including Ashdown House, Calcott in Buckinghamshire, Harrodian School, and 130 private schools.

Child abuse within educatin can also come in the form of bullying by peers or teachers, or both become complicit. Where dynamics are underhanded then it's often a child who becomes a target. Every child deserves to feel safe and while their parents should be willing to step in, should the need arise; measures should also be taken by schools to protect and create a safe, positive learning environment.

In further and higher education, there are cases of sexual misconduct on the part of lecturers. Many students have slept with the lecturers in attempt to gain higher marks, and this is often a result of the lecturer using marks as a controlling mechanism. When students don't feel like they are achieving much and ask their lecturer what they can do to improve their marks, some lecturers suggest sex as a way to improve their grade. This is clearly a form of sexual abuse. Lecturers taking advantage of any person trying to better his or herself is exploitation.

One example of such exploitation is in the case of Harriet Harman, who was working towards her political degree in the seventies; she had sex with the lecturer to get a grade of 2:1. This is still a common occurrence, and some younger students are advised to be an apprentice privately with the lecturer. If the lecturers are reported for their inappropriate behaviour, they may enact revenge, which will affect the student's ability to progress in life—keeping them from getting their chosen job, for example. This abuse of power is rife across all areas of further and higher education to this current day. The complaints system is too complicated for students in this predicament, and many drop out. Without a real audit to the reason why a student leaves, the abuse often goes unnoticed.

Numbers and Contacts

Below are some numbers and online resources for victims of child abuse:

1. The Survivors Trust (www.thesurvivortrust.org) offers counseling service for men, women, children, and victims and survivors.
2. One in Four offers a voice to support victims.
3. The Lantern Project (www.lanternproject.org.uk) helps survivors.
4. Women against Rape (www.womenagainstrape.net) helps asylum seekers who have suffered abuse.
5. 5Survivors UK (www.survivorsuk.org) helps male victims of rape and sexual abuse.

Lifecentre counselling service	0808-802-0808
Rape Crisis (www.rapecrisis.org.uk)	0808-802-9999
NAPAC (National Association for People Abused in Childhood)	0808-801-0331
NSPCC (National Society for the Prevention of Cruelty to Children)	0808-800-5000
Childline	0800-1111
Kidscape	0207-823-5430
Papyrus UK	0800-068-4141
Get Connected	0808-808-4994
MOSAC (Mothers of Sexually Abused Children)	0800-980-1958

Stop It Now	0808-1000-900
Safeline	0808-800-5008
RASAC (Rape and Sexual Abuse Centre)	0808-802-9999
Family Matters	01474-536-661
Child Helpline International	+31-20528-528-9625
Childhelp USA	1-800-422-4453

My Story of Child Abuse

There are many reflective questions survivors of child abuse ask when they reflect back, but abuse is never a child's fault. When I was seven years old, I was sexually abused by an adult male. I would walk home from school alone, and often the house would be locked. My neighbor would invite me over to stay in the dry and see his dogs until my parents got back.

After school I was invited over to his house many times and he began exposing himself. My parents were naturists, so it was not uncommon for me to see body parts. I never thought much about it when he started to expose himself. It made me uncomfortable, but it was no different in my mind than the naked bodies on the beach, which also made me, feel uncomfortable.

His perverse behavior increased over the weeks and months, where he would touch himself and make me touch him and then ejaculate into a glass and pour milk in it to drink. My thought at the time was that it was weird, but I never said anything, I kept my thoughts to myself. I didn't understand this at that age. When I was older and learned sex education at school, the penny dropped as to what had occurred years earlier, and I felt ashamed and embarrassed that he violated me and my trust in him. I felt sick. The mental shame I had felt lasted for years. When I told my mother, she didn't believe me, and I wasn't advised to go to the police. I felt like nobody believed what had happened.

Then at age fifteen, when again I was in a vulnerable situation, I was raped by the father of a friend I knew from school. This betrayal of trust and the physical violation compounded the previous trauma that I hadn't dealt with from my childhood. Being afflicted with such painful memories at such a young age had an incredible negative effect on me. I lost any sexual desire that maybe I should have had for my romantic relationship later, and intimacy was an issue, and the whole experience was unpleasant for many years after.

After the rape and child abuse, I was left with feelings of disgust and self blame. I did not have any physical bodily reaction at the time, yet the body and mind are intrinsically linked.

Fear and touch creates arousal, and it can also create haphephobia, so after my abuses I had no desire to go into a sexual relationship. I personally found nightclubs were like a meat market where people would frequent- just to pick a person up for sex. I really found this strange as I had no sex drive, and wondered how others can be driven by sex. Some people asked if I was gay but I had no desire at all, many people found this was a strange concept.

I became Asexual and some words and other people's actions created an adverse response, this triggered my flight response but I persevered in trying to get past the trauma. I was maybe considered frigid because I had no desire; however I still had sex because I wanted to be normal. Over the years I found my relationships were not working either and I even questioned how these past childhood violations could affect me so much and for such a long time on my sexual drive.

It took me several years to be able to forgive the perpetrators, (this was a challenge but as I moved in closer to God and away from these external influences it became easier). The traumas were affecting me less.

Reporting my trauma of child abuse was emotionally thwarted until I was in my thirties. However in my forties, I finally found closure. The rape case was eventually investigated properly. The closure made a huge impact on my mental health and I could let go of many repressed emotions: guilt and shame and take back my rights. It was empowering to feel less like a victim because I took the plunge to stand up to report it. I allowed myself to let go of any negativity.

CHAPTER 3

Dysfunctional Human Rights and Exploitation

Generally the poorer or more vulnerable a person is, the more exploited a person can be. Gas meters are more expensive than direct debit, loans are higher in interest. Higher purchases traps people in debt and poverty, and the list goes on. People have a right to be able to afford food (Article 25 of the 1948 Universal Declaration of Human Rights) as part of a right to an adequate standard of living (Article 11 of the 1966 International Covenant on Economic, Social and Cultural Rights). However, the exploitation of the poor and downtrodden is allowed to continue instead of the government providing adequate resources for people to live within these legal living standards.

Human rights abuse and exploitive abuse is the disrespect of a person's rights and freedoms, and yet this oppression of the poor still continues. Human rights include liberty, freedom of expression, right to food, right to work, and a right to education. All people have family rights and a right to safety. When people fall into this exploitive poverty trap, they often also fall victim to unscrupulous people who are happy to exploit victims for cheap labor, higher tariffs, sex or selling of body parts. Some predators just say its business and can often withhold funds or pay a lower tariff for labor, forcing people who have worked for that money to stay in debt and poverty. A perpetual cycle of modern day slavery completely disregards human rights and freedoms.

Often the most vulnerable are exploited, and there is no age that is immune to this exploitation. In many services and UK benefits system the people have been pushed over the brink leaving them to use food banks and take out loans with interest. Many of these persons are disabled and lone parents leaving them in a perilous situation. Complaints fall upon deaf ears, leaving many people with less people to turn to. This is often exasperated by the local government who send bailiffs to collect money for not paying local government bills (council tax) which incurs more fees, (bailiff fees) when they can't pay their bill already. I personally have always found this sadistic and cruel. Poor people are a vulnerable sect of society and yet there have been some barbaric actions from members of society against the poor. It is often not a lifestyle choice but often poverty is circumstantial.

In the UK, rent prices have increased so much that it often costs more than owning a home, and many don't earn enough to get a mortgage so many are trapped paying high rents all their life. Without owning a property this is going to create a massive black hole in the UK economy. Until people can exchange what they pay in rent prices/ funds into mortgage without a big deposit then the government will be faced with this future deficit, or no pension.

Too many vulnerable persons who are already high risk are pushed further into hardship and mental distress. Financial cuts, low wages, and escalating rents have created a myriad of suffering for the working person who doesn't own a home. One person in every 200 is homeless in the UK, according to Shelter, and 307,000 people are sleeping rough or have inadequate or temporary housing, such as hostels or bed and breakfasts. Shelter claims this is underestimated, as many are trapped as 'hidden homeless', who have nowhere to live but are not recorded as having a housing need. They end up 'sofa surfing'. VAWnet, a resource centre for national violence, wrote that there is no safe place for a homeless person and less for women. Homeless women can be coerced into sex at the hands of multiple perpetrators; 13 per cent of homeless women reported being raped in the last twelve months. There is no protection and no one to turn to. This totally violates the human rights laws to a safe place to live.

There are several reasons we have such high amount of homelessness: lack of affordable homes, minimum wage with ever increasing rents, no ability to save for a deposit that banks require, lack of family support. The universal credit, has contributed to homelessness and the surge in food banks, both which breach human rights.

In the UK and Hawaii there has been a failure to build enough affordable homes, both places are experiencing a surge of holiday homes with less affordable homes for the locals. There are more homeless than ever before, and more people are living in temporary housing, including families.

In general Europe, USA, Canada, Australia have cheaper houses except in Millionaires row, with lower rents and higher basic rate of pay in many of these. Visas are a potential issue however.

Being unable to afford rent and sleeping rough is now considered a criminal offence under UK law. I am not sure how this law stands against human rights laws.

An enquiry into the National Audit Office in September criticized the government for failing to get a grip on homelessness despite record numbers rising every year since 2010. Here are the statistics:

- In 2016/17, 59,000 households were accepted by the council as homeless. The numbers have been rising since 2009/10 to almost 50 per cent.
- According to the UK's independent fact-checking charity, 10,000 people were homeless and in need, but they have been deemed

intentionally homeless, in which case the local government does not help.

- In 2017, 4,800 people were sleeping rough in England. This is 15 per cent higher than in 2016 and more than double the estimate for 2018.
- Nearly 11,000 families were in temporary accommodation in September 2017, and 3,400 were families with young children, which is an increase of 3 per cent from the previous year.

Some have been waiting over fifteen years for a home. Not having a home in which to feel safe hinders development for children and can cause serious issues in their development. In 2017, 30,000 single-parent families were made homeless; a housing charity shelter reveals that three-fourths of homeless households are single-parent families who are working and juggling childcare with their work.

One report describes four women in four different circumstances who found themselves homeless. Some had well-paid jobs but became ill; one had dependent children. None of the women had a physical address, so they could not easily claim benefits, get jobs, or find any sense of security necessary to thrive. Even single men have been forced to return to the home of their parents or live on the streets because they are unable to afford the ever-increasing rent prices. The council has a responsibility to protect these people, but they more often decide that if a person becomes homeless, they have become so deliberately; therefore, the council will provide them with no support.

Some private landlords sell their properties, leaving families in a precarious position of looking for a home and packing their current belongings within two months. This situation has a detrimental effect on education and can have a negative effect on jobs as well. Shelter Housing Charity points out that the leading cause of homelessness is the ending of private tenancy and a combination of soaring rents and housing benefit cuts. Many landlords in the UK only allow a minimum term of six months; this doesn't provide security for children if they have to move every six months. The law was changed in the UK to prevent houses from being left empty; the government charges council tax on all properties from 2017. Previously, houses were left empty for long periods for capital investment.

Action Homeless is an organization which has teamed up with the Ministry for Housing, Communities and Local Government. Properties which are being left empty are being commandeered by local government and lent to some homeless people; often the homeless people need to renovate a disused property, but the situation nonetheless provides a home and safety where none was available before. The Empty Homes charity is an organization that highlights the extreme rate of homelessness and seeks 'to bring empty homes back into use'.

People without a home are judged ferociously; the man in the report for Action Homeless was unable to see his child for four years due to his housing situation. When families find themselves in poverty or homeless, they are unable to provide for their children and are deemed neglectful. Sometimes children are then sent into the care system for others with resources to adopt them. The adoption system is far from airtight and known pedophiles have managed to adopt children from the local government (council).

Mark Frost, known as Andrew Tracey, was a teacher who worked in different schools around the world and has been convicted of forty-five offences. He was a member of PIE (Pedophile Information Exchange, an international organization of people who trade in obscene material—often images of sexual acts with children) and a prolific pedophile. He managed to adopt a child from the council. This was highlighted by members of the public who knew of Andrew Tracey's history and change of name, and they alerted the authorities.

Questions are now asked about the checks conducted prior to adoption. Unfortunately, more children than ever are with these services because their parents are homeless and cannot provide for them, and it begs the question, why is it that when there are more cuts in benefits, there are more children in the system? The answer seems obvious and signifies a direct correlation between benefit cuts, homelessness, and children in the system. It would be more beneficial if the government provided enough funds to the families so that they could live in a home rather than put the children into care because the families struggle to cover the costs of food.

Children's Commissioner Anne Longfield said cuts of 60 per cent in preventative services since 2009 have effectively removed vital safety nets for at-risk youngsters and families, leaving them vulnerable to falling into extreme need. She states families have become marginalized, and the number of school exclusions have spiraled.

With child social services, initial child protection cases are up 73 per cent, which demonstrates a record number of children having child protection plans—75 per cent more than before the Baby P case in 2008. However, central government has reduced local authorities' cost by 40 per cent, and made cuts to benefits which affect poor working families, making them even more vulnerable. The main reason children are subject to child protection is neglect (48.1 per cent), and the secondary reason is emotional abuse (33.8 per cent). Ray Jones, a social worker and emeritus professor at Kingston University, says the universal credit system is not fit for purpose. This will leave families more vulnerable.

And even beyond the housing crisis, financial cuts to government-funded programs and basic benefits leaves young people particularly vulnerable. Financial cuts to certain disability benefits have allegedly amounted to more suicides in 2015/16. Lisa A. Goodman did a report in the American Journal of Orthopsychiatry (1991) that compared the difference between sexual and physical abuse in fifty poor housed mothers and the homeless ones. Both groups had been sexually abused, but the poor housed mothers had experienced more adult sexual abuse than the homeless; however, both had high prevalence rates.

In the USA, reports reveal that social institutions are not working effectively to prevent homelessness or protect vulnerable women. The people who work in the shelters are not trained to spot sexual abuse. The other issues in the USA are immigration with families and the splitting of children from their families;

The psychological damage could be profound; as written by Science Alert, the psychological damage caused by separating kids from their parents can be irreversible, which can lead to PTSD and an elevated risk of ongoing anxiety and depression. Using children to control parents mirrors domestic abuse behaviors.

In the UK 2018, It was observed in women's jails that most women in the UK are incarcerated due to being unable to afford their living costs. Such a statistic clearly reveals that women are victims of financial abuse despite Ministers who say you don't go to jail for not being able to pay bills. This breaches CEDAW, The convention on the elimination of all forms of discrimination against woman, this is an international treaty adopted in 1979 by the United Nations General Assembly, which is described as the international bill of rights for woman.

Another example of financial exploitation is the Grenfell Tower fire, where cheap hazardous materials were used on the external flats, this substituted cladding acted as a furnace when it caught fire. Over seventy people died in the fire. Cheaper materials were used in the construction to cut costs. The people living in the council flats were at the peril of the local council. The tenants had little control over the building materials used. Landlords, need to comply with human rights laws and provide a safe place to live. The local government has failed in its responsibility to uphold human rights, and so far, there have been no arrests or culprits held accountable for the deaths of those seventy people.

The law states that it is a human right to have a safe roof over your head and to have personal safety. Article 3 of the Universal Declaration of Human Rights says everyone has the right to live in freedom and safety (1948 UN Human Rights Act 1998 (the HRA)). Everyone has a fundamental human right to housing, which ensures access to a safe and affordable home with freedom from forced eviction. The right must be provided to all persons irrespective of income or access to economic resources.

Here are some resources available to people who may be experiencing human rights exploitation due to the corrupt, dysfunctional system:

Age Scotland	Scotland	0845-125-9732
Angus Women's Aid		01241-439457
Breathing Space		0800-83-85-87
Rape Crisis and Sexual Abuse Centre		01786-471771
Child Protection Line		0800-0223222
Debtline		0207-7553-7640
LGBT Helpline		0131-556-4049
Scotland's Domestic Abuse and Forces Marriage Helpline		0800-027-1234
Shelter Scotland		0808-800-4444
Samaritans		08457-90-90-90
Samaritans (Welsh line)	UK	0300-123-3011
Wales Domestic Abuse		0808-801-0800
SANEline		0300-304-7000
Calm Campaign against Living Miserably		0800-58-58-58
Mind		0300-123-3393
Papyrus UK		0800-068-4141

Anxiety UK		0844-477-5774
B-eat		0845-364-1414
Shelter		0808-800-4444
Centrepoint		0845-466-3400
National Call Center for Homeless Veterans	USA	1-877-424-3838
Help USA		212-400-7000
Mental Health USA		1-877-205-5681
Crisis Call Center		1-800-273-8255
National Suicide Prevention Lifeline (suicide helpline)		1-800-784-2433
Suicide prevention lifeline USA		1-800-273-8255
National Runaway Safeline		1-800-786-2929
Native American Suicide prevention		1-800- 273-8255
USA.gov		for housing and shelter, loans for homes, benefits
LifeLine New Zealand	New Zealand	09-5222-999
LifeLine Australia	Australia	1-300-13-11-14
National crisis line	Belgium	02-649-95-55
Canadian Mental Health Association crisis line	Canadian	250-426-8407
S.A.F.E.R.		604-675-3985
See all area hotline numbers		
Beijing Befrienders	China	03-5286-9090
Samaritans HK		2896-0000
Lifeline Shanghai		021-6279-8990
National crisis line	France	01-45-39-40-00
A Link with Life	India	91-44-2464-0050
Samaritans	Ireland	18-50-60-90-90
Childline		1-800-666-666

Rape Crisis and Sexual Abuse Centre		028-9024-9696
TELL Counselling	Japan	03-4550-1146
Lifeline		03-4550-1146
National crisis line	Netherlands Holland	0900-1450

My Life and Influences

My parents had their first child at seventeen, got married and started a business. In any business, there is an element of competitiveness, which I had learned from a young age and which would later support me in my business.

The eighties was an era of power and material possessions. My parents had acquired some wealth, and we were able to take regular holidays to the South France, as we had caravans in Saint Tropez. My sister and I would run around the campsite and go swimming in the sea, as it was located close to the beach. We learned to speak French as we would talk to the shop assistants to get a French stick and croissants. It didn't feel that my family was particularly different, except a little wealthier than the other children in my class at school.

When I was very young, my parents would often leave us in the house alone so they would go out to work. This was normal in the seventies. My sister (at age five) and I (at age 2) screamed the house down once when there had been a nest of tarantulas living in a banana box. The spiders had escaped and were in our bedroom. I vaguely remember this, but my sister was completely aware of the spiders; and every time she screamed, so did I. My neighbours had to break the door down as we were screaming so much. Then they found the gigantic spiders.

My sister and I were pretty independent for such young ages and totally unaware of any dangers. I only really saw my father on Sundays or at vacations, as he worked all hours. I didn't feel I needed to excel in school, as I thought I would end up working in the family businesses. My sister and I had helped daily after school and weekends, but seldom did we work in the same business venue until Christmas, and then it was all hands on deck. We packed as much as we could and as quick as we could.

In the eyes of every other person on our street, we were the perfect family. We had successful businesses, a nice car, were all dressed well, and took holidays abroad. But then the cracks started to appear. Our family unit started to break down, and when I was fourteen, my parents started their divorce, which became final when I was fifteen.

After the divorce, my sister moved in with her boyfriend and withdrew from her educational HND in Marine Engineering and Electronics course. I hadn't had the time to take any qualification as they didn't start until the following year. The next year I watched some kids with a similar school uniform on heading to school on a bus, while I wandered the streets aimlessly, I was unable to study without my book. I was always a studious arty child and handed my homework in, but there I was: I had dropped out of this system; it was very painful to be excluded for doing nothing wrong. I had no control over what happened to me. I was kicked down due to my circumstances, even though I was legally too young to rent. Sympathy fell by the wayside, and I was blamed for sofa surfing and I was unable to pay rent. People would say it was my choice and that I should get a job. I started an apprentice role, but it was low paying and wasn't even enough to cover my food. I became anorexic. But no matter how little I ate, I still couldn't afford rent. I ended up looking after children so I'd have a roof over my head and be in a fairly familiar environment for a while.

For years, I felt so negative. I cried every night for over a year. I had little control over my life. I can honestly say I could have died a thousand times over during these few years of my life. My life was so hard, and I never knew what would happen to me next. I had no protection and nowhere to go; I had no money, and I felt worthless. I couldn't even process my thoughts. All I could do was try to stay alive. Some people who knew I was vulnerable took advantage of me for their own gain and bullied me into situations because I couldn't do anything different. I still see young people nowadays facing similar ordeals that I had previously endured and wonder why there is so much homelessness and lack of support. So many live below the poverty line, and it's not what they have chosen. It's only their circumstances that dictated this, and I feel that more needs to be done to protect them and not leave these people open to exploitation.

I went to the local authorities for help, and they said I should go home. I explained I didn't have a home and that I was sofa surfing, but this wasn't their issue. The authorities did nothing. Trying to gain any normality at a young age was tough. On one hand, I spent years in school and was the straightest kid around, and then before I knew it, I had no home or money and was at the mercy of strangers.

I was raped and then groomed for sexual exploitation. There was nothing I could do to protect myself, as I was very vulnerable. I wasn't used to this way of life or had mixed with people outside school friends until now. I found myself in very challenging circumstances. I saw the underworld, the life most people will never get to see—not because I wanted to, but because that was where my life took me.

I felt like an orphan for most of the time and was very negative about myself. I was so impressionable and was bullied into situations that I didn't want to be in. I was manipulated and controlled by others and listened to what people said and took it literally; my sense of humor vanished, as did my soul.

I spent many years drifting and being complicit to other people's needs because I was looking to fill that void, but instead I became a victim time and time again. I thought that by helping everyone else, it would make me happy, but often I was just taken advantage of. The void was a big empty hole where my soul once sat. I used to have a totally different life, and when I was fifteen, my life just crumbled, never to be the same again. One trauma sat upon another, and this altered my sense of reality. I couldn't understand how humans could be so evil, and I didn't want to accept this because I had preferred the veil over my eyes, which protected me from these harsh realities.

I was exhausted, and I made little progress other than physically working longer hours and being more exploited. I was always too quick to try to please others and never looked at what I needed. But no matter how much I tried to make others happy, I still felt empty. My birthdays would pass by without even being noticed, and my twenty-first birthday was forgotten as many others. I didn't have the money to buy other people presents, so in return, they wouldn't buy me anything.

I was deliberately poisoned. I couldn't have certain foods, and when I was invited to have dinner, the food was laced with the foods I couldn't eat. I was repeatedly asked why I was still alive, why I have not caught AIDS or anything yet. Then I was told it was a good thing that I was not disabled as it would have been a lot harder for me. All these comments chipped away at me. If I was beaten, I was told I must have deserved it.

Years later I took some qualifications and kept plodding through life and used these skills to build a business. I developed my own business in my thirties and this was a saving grace for me. I didn't have time to listen to the toxic words and idle gossip. I was still experiencing bullying but it had a lesser impact on me. I closed the larger business when I was forty to bring up my child, and complete my degree however my resources had dropped considerably, and the lack of childcare also proved an issue.

Affordable childcare and the right to work is a human right CEDAW, and if I don't work I get money cut so much that I can't afford to eat, so this situation isn't easy, especially being a single parent. I struggled to find childcare weekends or after 6pm, so this was a challenge. I didn't have my financial independence that I had.

After doing my degree I met a professor who influenced me profoundly and made me question my belief system, he found me attractive and was very honest about me being aesthetically pleasing on the eye, and saw an inner beauty. Now that threw me and I spent a few months analyzing this and wondering why I was having issues accepting this so I reflected back on my life and saw I had experienced a lot of oppression, abuse, my rights disrespected and undermined which I had it drummed into me that "I should do as I am told", and "my thoughts are not even important" and if they want an opinion they will give it, and if I didn't do as I was told then I was bullied. I was subservient, and always to poor to buy new clothes or much; it was always about other people's gains.

Different comments had chipped away at my -self esteem, which I took to heart. I was told I had skinny chicken legs, too big of a bust, or that I was a skinny Cambodian (even though I am not Cambodian or skinny). I felt bad about my body and my voice, and how I said certain words, so I would stumble over my words and eventually refused to say anything at all. I had spent years trying to get approval and validation from others and working harder and harder, but this proved fruitless.

I did not know what limiting beliefs were or my belief system but this evoked my thoughts and I was processing this, reflecting and researching. Within this uneasy time of deep soul searching I severed all ties with many people. I didn't want my thoughts to be clouded by any influence, I didn't know what to believe, but I did know I had been through a lot of abuse, and spent years chasing the affections of people, and believed what others had said but yet I was struggling to believe the professor. He didn't want to take advantage or belittle me or want anything from me yet I was struggling with this.

I didn't want the influence of anyone, as I had to process my own thoughts and feelings and understand why I felt so negative about myself. This new direction that I took was what I consider to be reflecting and renewing. My solitude enriched my life beyond what I thought was possible.

The silence of my mind would be filled with clutter within seconds, and I needed to open the can of worms to resolve my negativity. It took several months of deep reflection and seeing my-self and all my faults and positives. I questioned everything—from my thoughts and feelings to my behavior and the impact I had on others and others had on me. I saw that I was a very accommodating person but not finance orientated, and I questioned why I was not. I questioned everything, and any unprocessed negative emotion I would process as well, no matter how hard. I enrolled on some psychology courses and I learnt some techniques to help me to help myself. This was a painful time for me processing all of it, and God became my best friend.

Since I stopped communication with most people it has protected me from verbal abuse. This helped me to set boundaries, and clearly see those who disrespect me. Some people are just toxic and evil.

I later joined some self-development activities that would support my personal growth. I was able to come to terms with some of the past traumas, and my confidence grew. I leaned on God as I felt more love and spiritually richer than before. For me, the church helped restore my soul, love, and self-esteem, which made me feel like I was enough and complete without requiring validation from others. This period of deep reflection led me to many discoveries.

CHAPTER 4

Domestic Violence, Sexual Abuse, and Rape

Domestic Abuse

Once you give your control away, you are at the mercy of another, which could be a hazard if the other person is abusive. Trying to leave a controlling person will prove dangerous. When you leave, they lose control. That is why I recommend you seek help from the police if you're experiencing this.

Domestic abuse can be perpetrated on male or female victims and is often a show of power and intimidation within intimate relationships, such as marriage, cohabitation, or dating. Often, the perpetrators are insecure. They may want to know where the victim is all the times and who they are with. When males get abused, it can be hard for them to talk about it, as society so often sees the males as the aggressors. This isn't always the case in relationships, and many men regress and try to escape the strong threshold of their abuser. It is the same for female victims as well. Domestic abuse has no sexual preference and can take on the form of more violent physical injuries as well as emotional, sexual, financial, controlling, verbal abuse; intimidation; threats; stalking; or gas lighting.

Humiliation is often something that occurs in front of other people to reduce the victim in the eyes of others and to create a diversion for other people to leave and avoid conflict. This allows the perpetrator full, undivided access to their target. It is about control over the other person, and this is not love. When the victim loses his or her self-confidence, it becomes easier for the perpetrator to gain more control. Physical abuse can develop after verbal abuse or humiliation has been initiated, leading to violence and physical assault or potential grievous bodily harm.

Domestic abuse that turns violent can be a destructive long-term battle. Physical injuries may subside, but emotional damage often lingers long after. Often victims forgive their perpetrators, as their feelings are clouded with love for this person who was supposed to be their life partner. Perpetrators can be very charming, which is part of their initial appeal, and this is why they become known as Jekyll-and-Hyde characters.

Physical threats or abuse is a way for some perpetrators to gain power— by planting the seed of fear in the victim's minds. A perpetrator can manipulate the victim's feeling of self-worth by undermining the victim's confidence and through different forms of abuse: emotional abuse, mental abuse, physical abuse, financial abuse, etc. An abuser may get angry for the smallest reason and point his or her finger at others rather than take responsibility for their actions.

There are a number of behaviors (red flags) to be wary of in emotionally charged situations:

- subtly insulting jibes
- snide remarks
- persistently finding faults (saying things like 'You look too fat in that')
- name-calling or shouting insults

- intimidation (acting like they would harm you, showing balled fists and visual glares)
- threats (even if they laugh it off as it's a joke, this is behaviour that can reduce the victim's self-worth)
- overt insults that lead to embarrassment in public (humiliation is meant to create submissiveness and to control the victim in the presence of others; this abuse is meant to push a person into subservience)
- stalking or gaslighting (a perpetrator will monitor their victim and watch more of the victim's life than the victim watches themselves; this can be a very threatening behaviour and can occur after a break-up or before any relationship has even begun between the perpetrator and the victim)
- sexual physical abuse or direct unwanted physical touch to the body (this can quickly evolve into rape, which is sex against the victim's will)

Sexual harassment is making unwanted physical advances on another person. Any unwanted touching to another person's body can be considered sexual harassment. Sexual harassment may start with touching an arm, and the person may not even notice. A female reporter at the World Cup who was groped and kissed on air spoke about the harassment to sports fans. Often, the people who object to this behavior are disrespecting the victim. They said, she is showing 'feminist hysteria'; however, this behavior is unwanted by the victim, and she should have every right to show her anger without being undermined. Some forms of sexual harassment can also include verbal sexual innuendos, verbalized.

Rape and the Sexual Offences Act 2003

Rape is often premeditated by the perpetrator. A perpetrator often rapes a person/victim they know personally, though serial rapists are often unknown to their victims. The victims often feel too ashamed to go to the police as they take on the guilt and shame for being raped or even drinking. Many people are date-raped by a perpetrator by using drugs against the victim to gain sexual control. Often, victims are completely unaware of this and just blame themselves for having one too many drinks but been unwittingly drugged. This happened to me when I was in my thirties. I was invited out by some other business colleague of my ex partner. I only had a sip of alcohol and then cola because I rarely drink and consider myself to be tee-total. He asked if I was abused as a child! Which I thought was a strange question to ask me. I just said, 'Yes, I was. How can you tell that?' and I mentioned that nobody has ever asked me this before. I didn't know he had spiked me at that point, but I knew there was something very different about me (totally out of character). He observed my new somewhat super confident behavior, as I starting singing and dancing on top of a table, I felt so weirdly confident, boiling hot and light headed. After about 30 minutes he grabbed me and pulled me in to a room and removed his clothes and mine. I could semi function but my body was limp, however verbally I could still talk and said his penis is tiny. He tries to rape me but he was having issues with my behavior as it was causing him to have an erection dysfunction. He became very agitated and told me to get dressed. I found it difficult to concentrate, putting my clothes on, and he dropped me off outside my home and just drove off quickly. I struggled to get indoors and I felt I could just sleep on my garden path but crawled indoors and I did pass out or slept for four days and had a fever after this. I didn't report it as he didn't rape me, and the whole ordeal was confusing and that is without alcohol.

Many vulnerable people who are homeless or in a disadvantaged position can become targets for serial rapists. In war situations or in situations where refugees are trying to seek shelter, people become victims of sexual abuse and rape. Many women are raped in war situations and become pregnant with their perpetrators' children. Often, these children are unwanted by the mother because of the nature of the conception, and sometimes the mother will put the child into a vulnerable situation from birth. A recent report states that the Rohingya fled to Myanmar and there have been widespread sexual assaults by the Burmese military. Hundreds of babies have been given up for adoption as a result of these assaults. This was also prevalent in Vietnam, where some USA soldiers were involved in sex crimes, in which they were sodomizing and raping women during the war.

Revenge porn is another form of abuse in this category. Revenge porn is a personal crime, and often the victim knows the perpetrator in an intimate way. With the breakdown of a relationship, a controlling partner may become vengeful and expose naked photos of their victim in attempt to humiliate them in public.

Revenge porn and ID theft is also used on strangers in date sites on the Internet.

Perpetrators, who charmingly demand intimate photos, often use these photos to blackmail the victim at a later date. The victim's innocently respond to the perpetrator's demands and are blackmailed at a later date. There are laws to protect victims against blackmail, including the Theft Act 1968. There are also laws to protect victims against the computer misuse (Computer Misuse Act 1990) if someone gets hold of their photo illegally. Other laws designed to protect victims of revenge porn are the Protection from Harassment Act 1997; the Public Order Act 1986; the Malicious Communications Act 1988; and the Human Rights Act 1998.

Domestic Violence

Controlling abusers are sometimes difficult to spot as they can seem genuinely interested in everything you are doing and simply make suggestions for improvement. Some red flags are: eliminate other people in your life whom they consider to be a threat, (often done in a tactful way or can be blatant) and start alienating you from your friends and family members. Abusers seek to create a situation in which you are entirely dependent on them. Their victims lose their own sense of worth or being; as they control their victims—even telling them how to dress. Controlling partners can play malicious mind games also to control their victims. In a patriarchal system, where men earn more than females, some men exhibit financial restraints over women; financial abuse is where the abuser watches how and when the victim spends money.

Physical abuse and humiliation are not limited to relationships; they can also happen in many settings, like in the workplace or care homes. There have been 2,400 reports of psychological abuse, 3,400 reports of physical abuse, and over 400 reports of sexual abuse in the UK. In the USA, the most common form of emotional abuse and humiliation happens in care homes. The American Public Health Association suggests 9 per cent or 2.5 million elders were abuse victims in care homes in 2016. Employers may also use physical abuse to control their workers. In the UK, many schools for learners with special needs have been caught on camera physically and emotionally abusing the learners. Care homes have also come under the scrutiny and some have closed after the evidence was put forward to the watchdog.

One other type of abuse I wish to discuss here is self-abuse. Self-abuse occurs when a person inflicts wounds or pain on himself or herself. A known case of self-abuse was that of Lady Diana. She described her experience as having feelings of self-loathing. Self-harm can also stem from neglect and a feeling of low or no self-worth. The internalized pain is expressed in injuring themselves. Victims need help to protect themselves from self-inflicting fatal wounds. Self-abuse has been on the rise in some schools, and investigations have been started in the North of England by Nigel Ward, the investigative journalist who writes for The Examiner. Ward has uncovered many cases and gaps in safety nets for victims of self-abuse. Self-abuse can also take the form of anorexia and bulimia, wounding, taking pills, etc.

Some abusive controllers are conditioned by their environment or culture in which abusive behavior has become the norm. This is more noticeable than ever before as more cultures integrate in society, then more issues surface. For example, labia mutilation, through medical observations, has become more recognized, and a greater awareness of this practice has come to the attention of health organizations in the world. FGM (female genital mutilation) is more prevalent in Africa, the Middle East, and Asia, but this procedure is a violation of human rights for girls and women. It is also an extreme form of discrimination against females. There are no benefits to this barbaric form of surgery, and laws have been implemented to rule this form of torture out. It is also a taboo subject for people to speak about genitals, and they have suffered in silence for years due to this.

Narcissists and sociopaths are potentially dangerous. A psychopath is dangerous by definition.

Narcissists are generally individuals who have their own agenda, but there are also cultures and families who share this destructive behavior against another member to ostracize and control them. Family 'wolf pack' behavior is often founded in their concept of bringing shame upon the family, which resides in the ego. The practice of honor killing or shame killing is often because a member has brought shame or dishonor to the family by violating religion or refusing to enter an arranged marriage or committing adultery. In some cultures, if a woman is raped, it is believed this brings shame to the family of the victim, which is often blamed on the woman. She may be killed as a scapegoat, while the real criminal is allowed to get away with their crime. Governments and police are trying to crack down on this draconian behavior by imprisoning the men who rape and maim women. There have been revenge killings, which occur if a person's reputation has been destroyed by a woman. The man may enact his revenge to restore the so-called balance in society and to save face. All these behaviors are ego eccentric and highly competitive and signify a lack of respect towards woman. Forced suicides are also dominant in south Turkey and Iran in order to conceal honor killings.

Below are helpline numbers and websites for rape and domestic violence support groups in some parts of the world. One thing to notice is that there are certainly more women-specific organizations across the world and less male-centered ones.

www.mensadviceline.org.uk

www.male-rape.org.uk

www.cxdv.org.uk (national centre for domestic abuse)

www.karmanirvana.org.uk (forced-marriages network) www.elderabuse. org.uk (elder abuse) www.rightsofwoman.org.uk

www.stalkinghelpline.org   www.respectphoneline.org.uk   (violent relationships) www.refuge.org.uk

Rape Crisis	Australia	02-9818-7357
Hilfe für Frauen in Krisen	Austria	43-316-82-77070
SOS Viol	Belgium	02-254-3636
Comunicacion y Vida	Brazil	115-543-6333
CAVAS	Chile	562-204-8886, 562-775-2684
White Circle Safety	Czech Republic, Prague	420-2-5731-7110
Women hotlines	China	8610-640-481-87
AMC	Costa Rica	506-233-5769
Dannerhuset	Denmark	45-3314-1676

The Open Door		45-3324-9103
Nucleus of Support for the Woman	Santiago	809-581-8301
Center for Group Support		809-530-3003
Fundacio Casa de Refugio	Ecuador	011-593-2-625-316
House of Eve	Egypt	202-3644-324
Rape and crisis centre	Finland	358-958-60-360
Paris Aide aux Victimes	France	0145-881800
Lara	Germany	2168888
CFSAW		0761-2858-85
DOVVSU (Domestic Violence and Victims Support Unit)	Ghana	233-021-662-438
Support centre for mistreated women		593-2-254-4662
CEIME	Greece	003-210-5242-733
Fundación Guatemala	Guatemala	502-475-3470
Defensoría de los Derechos de la Mujer		502-230-0874
Stigamot	Iceland	354-562-6868
VIVIDHA	India	911-413-921-48
Dublin Rape Crisis Centre	Ireland	1-800-778-888
ANTR	Italy	39-063-751-8261
Tokyo Rape Centre	Japan	813-320-736-92
Freedom House	Jordan	962-6-551-8421
Coalition on Violence against Women	Kenya	254-205-743-57
Woman Centre of Change	Malaysia	604-228-0342
CIDHAL	Mexico	52-777-318-2058

Sos	Holland	312-067-57575
Auckland Sexual Abuse	New Zealand	096-231-700
Oslo Crisis Centre for Women	Norway	22-37-4700
Program National Contra la Violencia	Peru	511-428-0569
Crisis Centre for Women	Russia	7-812-327-3000
Aware	Singapore	656-779-7137
Kwa Zulu Natal Network on Violence against Woman	South Africa	27-31-304-6928
Korea Sexual Violence Relief Centre	South Korea	822-338-7122
AADAS	Spain	915-740-101
BEDA	Sweden	460- 311-33-666
Women's Shelter	Switzerland	031-332-55-33
Taipei Women's Rescue Foundation	Taiwan	255-222-451-735
Concern for Development Initiatives in Africa	Tanzania	255-222-451-735
Turning Points (relief home and relief fund)	Thailand	929-2222
Purple Roof Women's Shelter Foundation	Turkey	212-292-523-132
Rape Crisis Centre	UK	0808-802-9999
Survivors UK		0203-5983898
Police		999
Family law line		0207-251-6577
Immigration and asylum line		0207-490-6562
Elder abuse		0808-808-8141

National stalking helpline		0808-802-0300
LGBT helpline		0300-999-5428
Revenge Porn Helpline		0345-6000-459
Women's national helpline		0800-222555
Research Centre for Family Health and Development	Venezuela	58-243-246-3796
	Vietnam	840-537-5700
National domestic violence and rape helpline	USA	1-800-799-7233

My Story of Sexual Abuse, Rape, and Domestic Abuse

I was sexually abused as a child at the age of seven and didn't realize that I had been violated until my lesson at school in sex education class; this left me feeling ashamed of my-self.

When I was thirteen, I went shopping in the city centre, which was about ten miles away. I got on to the bus and met my friend there, as she lived a few miles from me and on another bus route. On the way back from the city, I jumped on my bus after saying goodbye to my friend. Her bus approached first. As I approached my area, about a mile away, the bus just stopped, and the doors closed with the vacuum seal. I was the only passenger on the bus. There was another conductor, who came down from the upper deck and sat beside me. He put his arm around me, which made me feel very uneasy. He started to slobber all over me and touch me, and then he made light talk and asked my name and age. I was frozen and could barely speak; I told him I was thirteen! He looked shocked and said I looked older. He said he would open the doors and that he wanted me to run away as fast as I could. He walked to where the other conductor sat and opened the doors. I was about a mile from my home, but I knew where I was. The doors flew open, and I ran. The other conductor started to shout at the first, but I couldn't make out what he was saying because I was running for my life. Ever since then, I've had a difficult time riding public transport.

At fifteen, I found myself in a strange environment, sofa surfing on people's living room floors or settee—often with people I barely knew who had children. I would look after the children so I'd have somewhere to sleep. Sofa surfing was not what I was used to, and it felt like my childhood ended abruptly for me to be in that position. I was not fazed by hard work or looking after children.

Visiting the shops for some groceries on the sunny afternoon, I encountered a familiar face, my friend's father. I enquired about his son and family. He was driving and couldn't stop on the yellow lines and asked me to get in the car. I didn't know the city well and didn't drive my-self so I had no idea where he was driving; he said he can drive over to his sons which I thought would be nice to see some people I knew. He drove to his son, picked him up, and continued to drive. Later, he dropped off his son back at his mother's home and said he wanted to show me his new house. He drove into the square, and we walked into his gigantic house that had three floors. It was weirdly empty and cold and derelict on the ground floor. I went through the first door, and he locked the door behind us. I was feeling very uneasy as I looked around and there was an absence of furniture.

I remembered that this man used to practice witchcraft or said he did, and some memories came back to me of what he had said years previously; I generally switched off when people started talking about this because I was actually a Christian and witchcraft was intimidating to me. We walked up the stairs to the next floor, and he locked that door too. I was starting to feel pretty scared at that stage, there wasn't any furniture. Yet we continued to walk up to the next level. Then we reached the second floor, and he locked that door also once we were inside. We were at the top of the building, which overlooked a square. I looked out of the window, wondering how I can escape but I had an intense fear of heights.

I felt trapped and felt something wasn't quite right. It felt like everything was in slow motion—like it wasn't really me who was there. He walked into his kitchen and made a cup of tea and then came over and started kissing me. I was totally frozen in fear and still couldn't speak. He took off his trousers and pants. I couldn't move. I could feel I wanted to shout no! But nothing came out of my mouth. He pushed me on to the floor backwards, and he removed my clothes, which had popper buttons. I remained frozen, and he touched me all over and inserted his penis in me and started to push into me time and time again. I was like a corpse, unable to move. Then out of nowhere, I shouted for him to stop, but he didn't listen. He was hurting me—violently thrusting into me—and I shouted stop again and again. Eventually, he reluctantly stopped. I don't know if he ejaculated in me, but he did stop and told me to get dressed. He was angry but drove me to the barbican and just dropped me off in the street.

I had just been raped by my ex-boyfriend's father, and I was in mental turmoil. My life felt like it had turned into some kind of horror story, and I was just going through the motions, like it was a screenplay. I was completely in shock. I stumbled back to the flat where I was staying and couldn't say anything. The couple I was staying with was having their own issues and arguing so I went to the bathroom and had a shower. I didn't speak to them. I had nowhere to go. I was a quiet person who was brought up to speak only when spoken to, and I was emotionally struggling with what was happening to me. I seemed to have such little control over my life.

My mind was in total turmoil and I blamed myself because I thought I shouldn't have gotten into his car or been wearing a skirt with popper buttons and that I should have had lots of layers of clothes on, but these were irrational thoughts because it didn't really matter what I was wearing. He had one intention, and that was it. I was becoming dazed or void of any emotions except emotional pain.

I had done nothing wrong, but I felt like I was paying for some kind of bad karma that I didn't know about. I had always been a Miss Goody Two Shoes, but I was enduring these acts of horror. I cried nearly every night for God's help, but it felt like my cries fell on deaf ears.

I didn't go to the police after I was raped. I couldn't even tell the couple that I was staying with, who was an ex-CID officer, but the emotional pain was overwhelming. I questioned my own life and asked how my life had become so bad. I didn't go to the police until many years later, in 2013. The police conducted a thorough investigation, and they found the house where I was raped. The man had had a heart attack the year after he raped me, but the rapist's ex-wife knew or had a hunch something had happened and said he was an evil person. She and the policeman apologized. I could remove the guilt and pain I had held on to for so long and get closure.

With my healing, I now have closure, but I don't think the betrayal of trust is something easy to get over. I've forgiven the situation and myself for being in the wrong place at the wrong time. Some people are inheritably evil, and I do exercise more caution now than most other people. I have a heightened awareness in some situations, and sometimes my past trauma can create misjudgment, where my fear is heightened even though it's not necessarily a threatening situation. This has affected me for the long term psychologically.

You Give Me a Black Eye and Then Buy Me Flowers

When I was eighteen, I met a charismatic Italian, whom I was working with. He asked me out, and I said no—not because I didn't like him, but because I just wanted to be in my own space. He was pushy and asked again until I gave in and said yes. We started having a relationship by default. I wasn't in love with him, but he won me by charm. He would tell me he loved me more than anyone ever could love me, and I was needy for love. I had no idea that his actions were the start of controlling behavior; I also had no idea that my definition of love was different to his.

A few months went by, and when I became friends with one of the ladies from work, he became possessive over me. I went to work, and he interrogated me. He punched me several times in the face and body. I fell back on the door and hit my head and got bruised. I got up and was crying through the shock. He apologized and explained he didn't approve of my co-worker. He called her derogatory names, and I couldn't understand why he was being like this. I had no self-confidence or sense of self-worth, and I had been brought up to be compliant and to accept things and not question it. So I just accepted that he knew what he was talking about.

Before I met him, I had a tiny bedsit. When we got together, he said we could have a nice place if we put our money together. I accepted this. I thought it would be nice to have a better place to live, and I had no qualifications at that point or any other prospects, so I felt grateful that he would want to live with me. We rented a very nice penthouse apartment. He told me I could not have had this by myself, which was true because my wages wouldn't cover the cost of the flat, but his comments slowly chipped away at my autonomy until I thought I couldn't have anything without him.

He insulted my clothes, saying I looked like a tart and that my bag looked like a prostitute's bag. So he took me shopping to get me a new wardrobe. I started to feel like he was dressing me as a man. I wore clothes that I wasn't used to wearing, but I thought it was because he was Italian and obviously knew about design, so I accepted his suggestions. Then he told me how I should wear my hair. It was quicker to get ready, but I found the low ponytail he insisted I wear pretty boring. I am creative, but I followed his orders. Then he said I couldn't even walk down the street by myself and that he would walk with me and holds my hand all the time. I did think that was romantic rather than controlling at the time. I still felt needy for love and affection, but this relationship wasn't fulfilling this neediness that I felt.

I am pretty easy-going, but he would blow up in a rage if I didn't do what he told me to do. He would abuse me. The punches would fly, so I tried not to arouse his temper. We worked and lived together. I couldn't get away from him. I was often seen walking down the high street with black eyes and bruises, looking like I had been in a fight with Mike Tyson. But I never hit back. I tiptoed around to avoid confrontation. This man made me feel like he had done everything for me so I should be grateful. I was really good at karate as a child, but I didn't even try to fight back, because I didn't have any self-worth. I believed every word he told me. I didn't have friends, as he never liked anyone I got on with; he reinforced the fact that no one else wanted me and that I was lucky to have him as my boyfriend. I spent many occasions at the doctor with concussions; he sat right beside me, telling the doctor I fell off a chair or that I was painting and slipped. I was too scared to say anything to the contrary. I didn't think anyone would believe me because everyone thought so highly of him. If they questioned him, I feared that he would hit me for speaking out about it. So I stayed silent.

Everyone thought the sun shone out of him. He was always laughing and sociable, and many beautiful women would openly flirt with him. He wasn't short of admirers. Women saw he was always holding my hand and showering me with gifts, but the gifts were often meant as apologies for the abuse. He would say sorry and that it wouldn't happen again. But it did happen—again and again. I finally left him after several years. I just left as he went to the shops; I took my bag and left all my other possessions—never to return.

Two years later, I had felt or sensed he passed away or died and couldn't understand why I thought that. I didn't understand where this strange sensation was coming from, so I contacted the Italians and asked if they had heard form him. I hadn't been in contact for over a year with them as I had moved away, but they informed me he had died yesterday from leukaemia, which was in 1996.

As my ex died, I was actually involved with another man. Little did I know that the next boyfriend was just as violent, and after several times of being beaten up, my jaw was damaged. So I drove to the police station, and they suggested I drove to someone's house for my own safety. However, I didn't know that many people, so I slept in my car until I felt dirty and needed a wash and clean clothes. I went back to my abuser because I had nowhere else to go. I left him a few months after this, but I left most of my belongings again. I drove to a new area, about fifty miles away, to live,

For my safety, and I had to leave my job as my work said he was stalking the area and that I should not go in.

After having two violent relationships, I became very wary and wondered how I'd had two violent boyfriends. I questioned my own behavior. I wasn't unfaithful or did anything wrong, but this doubt in my mind led me to see that I was a people pleaser and I never looked at my needs. In fact, I didn't even know what I needed; as I had been too busy pleasing others and being subservient. I just wanted to be loved, and I was wondering why it is so difficult.

The long of the short for me was, I was looking externally for approval and love rather than building or developing any self-esteem. I had abandonment issues and inner conflict. I was looking for love externally and for someone to protect me. This made me very vulnerable. When I became involved in a relationship, I felt thankful someone loved me and was there for me, which was probably because I missed the security and the feeling of safety. This was my own ideology—that my boyfriend would protect me. However, the truth was far from my own ideology, and I was being beaten.

I wanted to believe they were looking out for me, but the truth was, they were only doing that to control me and use me for their own benefit—without any love. I did what they said and not what I liked, and I hadn't any outside interests. I had no life or hobbies outside the relationship. I didn't even have fun in my relationships, and not once did we laugh and enjoy our day in all those years. Their control was built on my own insecurities and my lack of knowledge of what love and happy relationships are supposed to be. I lived in fear for most of the time, being left destitute, and then ironically, I left them with nothing. The fear of being constantly beaten far outweighed having nothing. I didn't have any qualifications and couldn't get a job easily due to this, and I had another fear of getting qualifications. This whole situation left me vulnerable and susceptible to being controlled.

I cleaned the house and made dinner for them so it would make life easier for them. I actually became more like a slave and forgot who I was. If they didn't like church, then I didn't go. If they didn't want to go to the cinema, we didn't go, and I was too scared to go by myself because of my previous negative experiences of rape and traumas. My mind was filled with fear, and I didn't feel safe; hence, I wanted a boyfriend to protect me. I saw their possessiveness as being protective; however, they didn't protect me physically and they mentally abused me. I thought that if I tried harder, they would love me and treat me better, but this wasn't happening. Instead I became a doormat and their punching bag.

In hindsight, I wasn't even ready for a relationship. I needed to be happy with myself. My self-esteem was really low, and this led to my own insecurities, which was unhealthy. I found I was too busy being a people pleaser that I didn't even look at my own needs. I needed love, but I mistook possessiveness for protection. They wanted sex, so I had sex with them; however, this wasn't even enjoyable. After I had sex with them, I felt committed to them, and that in itself was like glue. My faithfulness was challenged even more when I decided to walk away several years later to end the relationship. I needed to feel secure in myself before entering another relationship. As much as I desired commitment, there was little point in committing to the wrong person, so I needed to work on me being happy without anyone else. I needed to drop all expectations and norms, and people's opinions because this took me away from my authenticity. I needed to value myself more, so this was an area of my personal development that I had to work on. However I didn't come to that realization for many years.

I needed to protect myself, and by not having any sex before marriage, this helped me to identify those who would string me along to those who were serious. Many would not be interested if I wasn't prepared to have sex with them. Not having sex provides more trust, and you won't ever feel insecure or jealous over anyone else because you know they're willing to wait. I still feel marriage is right for me.

The place where I was raped

CHAPTER 5

Human Trafficking

Human trafficking is the complete exploitation of, often a vulnerable person. Many gangs and pimps try to befriend their victims; they talk them into a situation that sounds very nice and supportive for the victim. The abuser then violates the victim's trust and manipulates the victim into an unsafe situation.

The biggest platform for abuse of this kind is the social media. Online, a predator can tap into a child's or victim's page and befriend him or her and all of his or her friends. Slowly, predators groom their victims; they charm them with kind words or buy them things or send them suggestive icons on social media. The predator often uses a false identity. Over time, their communication may move to the phone or a different medium in order to get the victim away from their safe zone and into another zone where the predator can gauge how impressionable the victim is.

Many young people have been groomed and are not even aware of it until they reach the perpetrator's chosen destination and are abused. Many assume trafficking only occurs abroad, but there are many cases in the UK, or home turf and in almost every city. A predator often grooms victims for a while, either online or directly in some settings. They may charm the victim to gain their trust or cultivate a fake love affair so the victim becomes compliant and fooled. Whilst perpetrators are communicating they are concocting a deceitful plan towards their victims, before leading them to their demise of abuse, they may find out a lot of information on the victim, such as how they look, where they live, and whether or not they are wealthy. Wealthy people are generally less vulnerable to trafficking, but perpetrators may try to exploit the family for money. Predators may also sell their victims to other gang members who may mark the victim with their brand, tattoo.

Child exploitation and online protection centers estimate 300 children are victims of trafficking in the UK every year. Women are also trafficked and may be sold to a gang to work in the sex trade. Many victims are promised a better life—such as being promised a job. Victims don't realize they are being groomed. Trafficking is a vile trade, and the most saturated area for victims is in Europe. Under the Children Act 1989, it is the council's legal responsibly to care for children under the age of eighteen who are brought to their attention. He or she is supposed to be placed under care if the child is unaccompanied by an adult or if the parent of the child is unable to care for him or her—for example, the child and parents are homeless. However, the councils are failing with housing, leaving many families and children vulnerable. Even now there are surplus children living in homeless situations and have been staying in temporary housing for years.

Various cuts in protection services compromise the safety of the people. Some council has outsourced services such as childcare, which allows anyone to have access to offer their services. Anyone can enter their details on paid sites. Some childcare providers don't have any police checks. The council's decision to outsource the services has created a plethora of vulnerable people. It's an easy way for a pedophile to acquire children by offering these services undetected.

If councils provided a 24/7 childcare service in registered settings it would protect families and offer more nurses, and shift working parents the opportunity to work any hour securely.

The police and Interpol are working, trying to prevent human trafficking. Trafficking has become prolific in countries such as Thailand and Vietnam as well as East Europe and the USA. Often victims are trafficked for a predator's financial gain. Due to some of the perpetrators position in society it can be very close nit, where they often defend each other and protect their own interest at the expensive of a victim. It will continue to be difficult to prevent trafficking and abductions.

There are thousands of migrants around the world currently fleeing their own countries to seek refuge and safety. Trafficking is a serious issue for the vulnerable migrants, many are abducted and trafficked, a big case was in 2018, Greece where children were trafficked for the purpose of body organs. Women are also sold into brothels or prostitution and are too ashamed to speak out. Children are also made to work in many industries for little pay. These are often trapped for many years.

I am alive to tell my story, and I know the paralyzing fear that occurs when you are abducted and trafficked. Speaking out and standing up against these criminals is difficult and terrifying. Often, cases of trafficking are linked to large networks of organized criminals. The law still has a long way to go to understand that the victims are often silenced and fear reprisals. Seldom do victims take gangs to court due to the fact the law often penalize the victims and are given a criminal record for soliciting when they have been the victim of crime.

Criminals know exactly what they are looking for and are often in positions of authority over their victims. Victims are often misled to building up a trust with a perpetrator, this betrayal of trust impacts the victims inability to trust in their future. It is often very difficult for victims of trafficking to trust authority figures and officials after being abducted or trafficked.

Below are some laws that have to do with trafficking:

- Trafficking Victims Protection Act (TVPA) of 2000

- Trafficking Victims Protection Reauthorization Act of 2003
- Trafficking Victims Protection Reauthorization Act of 2005
- Trafficking Victims Protection Reauthorization Act of 2008
- Trafficking Victims Protection Reauthorization Act of 2013
- Justice for Victims of Trafficking Act (JVTA) of 2015
- Preventing Sex Trafficking and Strengthening Families of Act 2014
- Modern Slavery Act 2015
- Section 59A of the Sexual Offences Act 2003
- Trafficking people for labour and other exploitation (2004 act)
- Criminal Law Act 1977
- Serious Crime Act 2015
- Fraud Act 2006
- Children and Young Persons Act 1933
- Theft Act 1978
- Child Abduction Act 1984
- Sexual Offences Act 2003
- Criminal Justice Act 2003

What happens to victims of trafficking? According to the UK tracing service, 200 people are found murdered. Most end up being shipped to Belgium, which is the capital of human trafficking of children and women. Children disappear and are never heard from or seen again. India also has high statistics of women who go missing. Many are said to have mental health issues and have committed suicide. One in five are said to have mental health issues in the UK. According to National Crime Statistics, an average of 58,000 people is abducted by non-family members. Also, 115 victims are kidnapped and held to ransom. In the US and UK, 1 million children are reported missing every year. In England, 275,000 people went missing in 2009. According to National Crime Agency, 335,000 people in England went missing in 2015. In Germany, 50,000 people went missing; in Brazil, 40,000; and in France, 39,000. Some were found to be part of a cult, but it was only a small number who were found dead in a circle position. In Australia, 30,000 people went missing; in Spain, 8,400; and in Italy, 1,100. These numbers make it clear that trafficking is a rampant worldwide issue.

People are often targeted by gangs as well. Chief Superintendent Sharon Kerr, who heads Scotland Yard, said serious and organized crime units have led to increasingly complex and high-risk situations. Gangs are using different methodologies to abduct their victims. Operation Welby was a torture, kidnap, and drugs case, but the victim refused to give evidence. Operation Scottow was a case that included child abduction and the ransom of a child. The perpetrators were jailed for kidnap, blackmail, and false imprisonment. Operation Runman was where a businessman was abducted and held for ransom. His wrists and ankles were tied up with tape, and his arms were pinned to his body. Tape was put over his eyes and mouth. Cases such as this are on the rise.

Below is a list of missing-person helpline numbers:

UK	116-000
Australia	00-61-011-800-0843-5678
Canada	001-800-843-5678
EU	00-800-0843-5678
Hong Kong	00-852-022-800-0843-5678
Japan	00-81-011-800-0843-5678
Mexico	00-52-001-800-843-5678
USA	1800-843-5678

Contact Helpline Numbers	
Salvation Army	0300-3038-151
The Modern Day Slavery Foundation	0800 0121 700
NSPCC child helpline	0808-8005-000
Police	999
Crime stoppers	0800-555-111
Child suicide mental health helpline	0800-068-4141

Childline	0800-111
Reunite International Child Abduction	(0) 1162-556-234
Adult suicide	0300-111-0101
Anti Terrorist hotline	0800-789-321

Groomed and Trafficked

Many forms of grooming happen in broad daylight and are so subtle that unless you had been groomed or trafficked, then you could be oblivious to any signs. Many types of slavery happen under our nose, and yet the majority of people are so busy hitting their personal work targets that they don't notice anything that doesn't concern them. With the governmental cuts, it will create more vulnerable persons, and this is where gang masters will soar in profit at the expense of the vulnerable.

In early teenage years, most children are in school and living at home, but those who are not are at a disadvantage or vulnerable. Of course, most people at this age are totally unaware of the hazards that lurk around them, and there is little guidance if people cannot fulfill what has been stipulated by government rules. I still see local children who have been struck off school due to their behavior needs, and not have any education at all for over two years. These children just sit in their homes or roam the streets, however if a child who is currently at school goes on holiday and misses a few days off school, then parents can be fined 2000! This is double standards.

I was in a similar position when I was fifteen. I thought I was street-wise and but this couldn't be further from the truth. I was sofa surfing and looking after other people's children due to my circumstances, and I was too young to rent an apartment or get financial help. So I traded my skills for a roof over my head and a meal. Often I would sleep on the settee, which is now known as sofa surfing. Many of the children's parents were poor and couldn't afford to eat properly. They were exhausted from working and bringing up their children, so often I would take the children out to give the parent's time to rest. Other parents just needed extra help with tidying and cooking, but they couldn't afford to pay me.

Most of the children who I had looked after lived in a low-key estate. The parents were exhausted from working and often couldn't even afford help. Everyone and anyone live in the estates and often the local authorities place ex offenders in a home within these estates, these included sex offenders and people straight out of jail. Many sex offenders are apparently deemed safe with children, but there are several who are not.

One of the parents from where I had been staying moved to another low-key estate where a past convicted pedophile had stalked the child and murdered her. After that happened, I realized that these housing environments were stalking grounds for predators. It was easy access to vulnerable people who had little protection. At any point, a child could be abducted or trafficked. Not even I could fully understand these dangers, at such a young age. How unaware I was of my own situation.

As I was child minding, I met a talkative man. He knew I didn't have a fixed home and asked if I wanted to move in with him. I never saw any risks, and I guess that was down to my Asperger's and the fact I had been sofa surfing in many parents houses. I did move in with him, but after a short time, he declared his undying love for me and wanted me to have his child. I didn't feel comfortable having a child in my teenage years, so I said no. I was in a precarious situation, and I was talked into doing things which made me feel uncomfortable. So when he introduced me to his friends who had a baby, I offered my services and moved in with them rather quickly, to never see him again.

The new couple that I had moved in with was very sociable and busy. The husband asked if I would work in his new workplace as a secretary, with a wage, instead of being a child minder. I agreed, but I struggled with this job as I was dyslexic, (however I never found out I was dyslexic until I was 40). I stayed here for several months. In the summer I went to the shops close by and saw my friend's father, who later raped me that day. I went back to the couple's place after that ordeal that day and stayed silent. The couple was having issues, and introduced me to a drug dealer who they suggested I stayed with for a while. I knew nothing about drugs. They would pick me up a few days later, or the next day if I was working. This went on for many weeks.

The drug dealer then declared his love for me, and this made me feel uncomfortable, and the whole situation. I had always been sporty and arty, precise with detail. I wasn't used to this bohemian lifestyle, and I didn't want to get used to it. I didn't know what I was doing in that situation or why I was there, as this was so different to whom I am. They treated me nicely, but I didn't ever want to be on the back of a motorbike, mentally floating from all the fumes that were in the house. I was quite happy in the fresh air with the birds chirping and quiet surroundings with art or creating clothes, Jewellery designs or doing cosmetics. I loved the eighties era, and now I was in a totally unfamiliar environment. It was kind that they put me up but I didn't want to be there.

I went back to the couple again and met a gregarious woman who offered me another job. This appealed to me as she said it was window display work. I had left school before I wanted to and had no hope of getting any qualifications, so the thought of being offered this was amazing. I could finally use my creative talents. I was an A student in art, and I knew she wouldn't be disappointed in my work. I felt happier, I felt like life was getting better. She came to the house many times and spoke about the job but not in great detail; the conversation was more about when I should start my new job. She asked if I had a passport, but I didn't, so she was going to obtain a passport for me, which I thought was very kind of her. I was going to Holland. I had been to Vollandam on a school trip previously and found that it was a very beautiful country, with many fields of tulips.

She talked about my earning potential, and money in a way that induced familiar memories and this grated with me, so I would stop listening to the lady. The subject of money roused my self-defense mechanism. The lady came to the couple's home many times; she sorted my passport and mentioned the date of the ferry, which I forgot! I was reminiscing on my school friends and school. This brought back incredible sadness, and I started getting panic attacks and anxiety. I also missed my family and then decided to walk to where my father worked. He had just bought a house from saving up after the divorce and he said I could stay there; I had a distant relationship with him as he had always worked a lot, but I decided to stay there.

I walked to work from my father's, and on the way home from work, I met some of the people from the estate. They asked me to go into a pub, so I had a soft drink, I was thinking that I am in a pub and yet my old school friends are in school, this didn't sit comfortably with me.

I walked home by myself, and I woke up the next day in my father's house, semi-naked on the sitting room floor, unable to move. The police were standing over me, and the man who was looking after the house was crying. The door was all smashed in, and a lot of my father's possessions were stolen. I had no idea what had happened or how long I was unconscious for. The police found who did it, as one of the neighbors reported it, but to this day, I have no memory of what happened.

After that, I felt really bad for my father. I decided not to go to Holland and I didn't even see her to tell her, I changed my mind, I gave up my job. I was scared to walk to work and of these people. I moved into my own bedsit on the other side of the city on my seventeenth birthday, when I was legally old enough to rent my own place. I got a new job in a factory that paid more for my age, which enabled me to pay my rent and buy food. I was able to have some independence, which made me less reliable upon others and less vulnerable as well.

Months later, I found out the window display job was prostitution. I was actually being groomed, to be trafficked to Holland and work in a brothel, but I was completely unaware of this. The woman was trying to trick me so she could easily abduct me and force me to work as a prostitute when I was in Holland. I thought the red-light district was a fashion area and that I was going to be doing window display work. It was fortunate that I was reminiscing about my school and family and that I went to visit my father, or I could have been another statistic. I dare say the drug dealer kept saying he loved me in attempt to line me up to be his mule.

This experience or trauma has been like a thorn in my side for most my entire existence, plagued with mental trauma and fears up until I was in my 40s, I didn't know this had affected me so much until I reflected in my journal, and then I had a revelation that this trauma was the root cause of my agoraphobia, and fear of people. So it meant I could pray and work through this issue.

The estate where I would look after some children

CHAPTER 6

Scams

Every day we are bombarded with letters and emails and, of course, the telephone sales calls or men calling from India, telling us our computer has a problem whether you have a computer or not. There are so many ways people can get scammed over the phone and on the Internet—through phishing emails that have virus lottery, Student Finance England, Paypal, gaming, fake goods, ID, education courses, date sites through many fake sites, and even scam artists using genuine sites. There are also reputable companies who scam their customers—Big banking giants perpetrate scams and now we have PPI, and it seems everybody is in on it now and crossing over to the dark side. I don't think it's morally right to take advantage of other people, and therefore, I include scams as a form of abuse.

Scams occur when you think you're going to get something for which you pay a fee but actually get nothing. Unfortunately, victim often lose money and can't get it back.

Identity theft is another scam, forms of ID : passport, bank details and photo ID. Scammers are often ruthless and leave can victims broken.

Very few people are immune to some form of scam and some are more vulnerable, such as widows, single parents, learning needs, single people, or elderly people.

As a society, we need to change; we are constantly becoming more and more divided, and certain groups are ostracized, leaving them vulnerable to scams.

Some people have lost their life savings as a result of scams. This causes the person to be further isolated. Some examples of scamming cases are listed below:

- There have been a couple of stings in New York where men were putting their details out on date sites and conning women out of $100,000.
- The Microsoft scam was where a caller calls you, telling there is something wrong with your PC. The scammers would get the victims to download a virus or malware for a fee. The culprits were caught in July 2017 and eventually arrested in the UK.
- In the O2 scam, staff members tricked customers into signing contracts for a huge commission. The whistle-blower informed The Sun paper, and the company was made to cancel unwanted contracts.
- The TalkTalk customers scam was found to be on an industrious scale, with sixty employees contacting TalkTalk customers, perpetuating cyberattacks.
- Builders have for several years been subject to the watchdog for bodge jobs or simply not turning up to do the work after being paid, but there has also been a case of computer hacking in which victims were conned into thinking they were sending money to the builder over email but the email was hacked by the scam artist, who took the money. This particular case was reported by Kevin Peachey, personal finance reporter of BBC ('Scammers Struck as My Mum Was Dying', 16 June 2018).
- In India, newspapers advertise jobs in call centres, some of which are meant to scam people. One man reported that he called unsuspecting people in America to say they were under

federal investigation for tax evasion and left a number to call back if he hadn't talked directly to the victims. These conmen were reading a script given to them and getting paid a wage. The whistle-blower in this case contacted The Guardian and said he just needed a job but didn't like the way he was being treated by his employer. He therefore explained what he was being paid to do, and it turned out to be a scam.

Unfortunately, many of these scams are based abroad and prey on victims in a different country, which makes investigation extremely difficult without the intervention of Interpol.

Below are numbers to call if you fall victim to a scam:

- police in your country (first you should contact)
- Citizens Advice: 0345-404-0506
- Financial Ombudsman: 0800-023-4567
- watchdog: 03700-100-222
- Action Fraud: 0300-123-2040
- National Trading Standards: 03454-04-05-06

Don't even try it!

I come across the same scams as everyone else. I receive phishing emails and letters trying to extract money out of me. Or I get advertisements for fake education centers who are selling courses with an ulterior motive, often to obtain a UK visa.

I got caught on social media. I was addressing an issue on a political page, and a man commented also. The conversation flowed back and forth and then he sent me a friend request, so I added him and didn't think much of it.

He soon put me on this pedestal and laid it on strong; he even started calling me many times on the app throughout the day. I found this very unnerving, but I justified this behavior by thinking he wasn't doing any harm. He asked for my domestic address, claiming he wanted to send a present, but I didn't feel comfortable with that. He later demanded money for the courier service and came up with an extremely lame story. I explained I never even wanted a present so I am paying for nothing.

After an apology from him, he had explained he had been stress due to his hotel! A story started to form, like he was reading it off a script. He wanted to transfer money into my account so that I could choose the decorations for his new hotel, and he wanted me (a stranger who he had never met) to run this large hotel.

I got a call the next day from a man with a South African Accent, saying he was from the bank and wanted to transfer money to my account and asked me for £500 holding deposit. I told him I was busy and to send an email (thinking he wouldn't). The email came through with an invoice on letter headed bank invoice.

I was getting agitated as I didn't want thousands put into my account.(I have a phobia of money) so I phoned the number on the letter headed paper and I explained that I was not happy about money going into my account, and asked to speak with the man, who contacted me a few moments ago. The lady mentioned it couldn't have been this man as he was the CEO in Hong Kong and hadn't been in Europe.

The CEO was Japanese and did not have an African accent like the man had who phoned me earlier. The bank numbers were genuine, but had been stolen. The account details were of the CEO, his account had been compromised and under investigation.

I was totally shocked at the openness from the bank and of this information.

The African man called the next day, completely unaware that I had talked to the bank, so I played along. He asked me for the funds, and I told him I tried to transfer the funds but it came up with an error message. I said maybe he needed to check it. He gave me another account and then another. I had over seven bank account numbers that they were using all across the globe. The bank numbers and codes were all genuine; I checked them with the bank, and they all belonged to someone. These accounts were actually hacked by the conmen, and they were laundering money. I then wondered how many people were involved in this scam, so I checked the social media and delved deeper.

I noticed I was getting a lot of unknown people popping up on my profile, wanting me to add them. I vetted the profiles and noticed some similarities in wording, and then I looked at who was on their page. I clicked through the people listed on their friend's lists, which was limited, and covertly asked for some details, to get a bigger picture. I asked how long they had known there friend. Many were swept away by the charm and were expecting a parcel! I asked more and they had sent money for a parcel which never turned up. I found out many of these women were sending money. Some lost between £600 and £2,000 each.

I then ran the photos through the search engine, to match the true identity, in Google. The entire lot of photo IDs were stolen.

Each victim was led by a story, and showed me some of their messages, all with similar wording, like queen, babe, and sugar, (where these words incidentally irritate me) and had phone numbers which was the exact same contact number as the African man had given me. I went to the fraud department but as it was an African number then it was out of UK territory.

I contacted the real people, whose photo ID had been compromised to inform them of the situation as to make them aware. One of the photo IDs that was stolen was of a Bishop in USA, and I watch his services. Most of the victims reported the conmen to the social media platform, and made several attempts to have him or them stopped.

CHAPTER 7

Discrimination and Financial Abuse

Heaven and Hell: The Parable of the Long Spoon

One day a man said to God, "God, I would like to know what Heaven and Hell are like."

God showed the man two doors. Inside the first one, in the middle of the room, was a large round table with a large pot of stew. It smelled delicious and made the man's mouth water, but the people sitting around the table were thin and sickly. They appeared to be famished. They were each holding spoons with very long handles and each found it possible to reach into the pot of stew and take a spoonful, but because the handle was longer than their arms, they could not get the spoons back into their mouths. The man shuddered at the sight of their misery and suffering. God said, "You have seen Hell."

Behind the second door, the room appeared exactly the same. There was the large round table with the large pot of wonderful stew that made the man's mouth water. The people had the same long-handled spoons, but they were well nourished and plump, laughing and talking.

The man said, "I don't understand."

God smiled. It is simple, he said, Love only requires one skill. These people learned early on to share and feed one another. While the greedy only think of themselves...

Sometimes, thinking solely of our personal gratification, we tend to forget our interdependence with everyone and everything around us, so much so that we stop caring about them. But, as the parable makes it clear, by doing so, not only don't we help others overcome their suffering, but we're also unconsciously harming ourselves, since we are all connected on a very deep level.

Financial abuse is taking advantage of someone who has less power for financial gains. Financial abuse may take the form of a higher cost for services. It may even take the form of unfair loan agreements in which the person who has loaned money has to pay an unfair amount back in interest. All these services cost more than it does for others who have adequate resources. It costs a poorer person more money to attain these services because of all the sanctions and barriers companies impose. Service providers make more profit from these implementations, but it is morally wrong to do such a thing to as it holds people back in life. It traps people in a situation where they pay more and they have lesser chances in life. Poor people are often the most discriminated against, suggested by Anne Firth in Stanford University.

Financial abuse is a form of control which suppresses and leaving them struggle in their lives with debt and poverty.

Here are some examples of discrimination and is not exhaustive: All discrimination is illegal The Equality Act 2010

- Direct Discrimination :
- Indirect Discrimination:
- Pregnancy: and loss of jobs, finance.
- Age: Often elderly and young

- Sexual Orientation: Gender preference
- Race: Some think they are more superior
- Religion: A Belief system
- Workplace: pecking orders discriminate
- Housing rents: becoming unaffordable, children, animals
- Insurance companies: young drivers, house insurance for tenants
- Poverty- and wages being lower than others for the same job
- Single Parents- Costs, holiday deals, mortgages
- Law: When perpetrator can afford a good barrister against the victim
- Gender – see CEDAW laws
- Financial- wages between the sexes, scrutinizing how a partner is spending the money.
- Travel Tax- surcharges in peak times to exploit often families
- Childcare-no set price and can be open to exploitation
- Care and support: wages low, care expensive
- Bank cards- interest high for poorer people
- Loans: interest
- Legal support: unfair for poor people
- Fat cat pay: perks to select persons
- Mortgages: against working families who haven't got a deposit
- Disability: equipment required and not always obtained, aids to help the person with the disability are not always affordable. Communication needs and learning needs.
- Pip: This is a very strange benefit for people who are disabled but some people with autism, learning needs, mental health struggle to get any support even though the doctor states they are disabled.
- Universal credit: in the UK has brought severe hardship to those often working and most in need. This has caused to attend food banks in order to survive. This effects the poorest and neediest in society.

Financial abuse and exploitation, not exhaustive list

- Blackmail : verbally or financially holding another person debt
- Bribery: Use to manipulate into a the brides favor
- Cheap Labor: Exploiting a person for financial gain

Council turning away vulnerable persons: The council has duty of care under the care legislations.

- Trafficking: Drugs or people for financial gain
- Silence payment: In 1992, the Catholic dioceses in the US paid out thousands to settle hundreds of sexual abuse cases. This is called hush money or silence payment, which is meant to keep the victims quiet. The victims signed a non-disclosure agreement and were given money to keep their abuse stories quiet. The Vatican was aware that the church paid this large sum of money to silence its victims. Silence payment is a form of bribery to save a corporation's or church's reputation or as a cover-up for something worse to avoid a bigger investigation. Ray Mouton, a lawyer the church hired in 1985 to defend a pedophile priest in Louisiana, was warned of the consequences of not supporting the victims. The pedophile needed to be removed from the church leadership position. The case eventually cost the church $2.6 billion in 2006.
- Law and legal loopholes and tax havens: Hiding money in offshore. Some people may think they earn it and why should they pay tax? Well many people work for minimum wage and people who exploit loop holes often live the life on the backs of other people hard graft. It's not really fair.
- Laws: people flouting laws at the expense of damaging another person's life.
- Laws: We have different laws in the UK which seems to undermine criminal law.

- Local government rules: Doesn't support a person if they can't afford rent and are made homeless yet international law says everyone is entitled to a safe home and able to afford food.
- Government: Not paying pip for disabled person, as the government criteria is discriminatory which breaches human rights against disabled people.
- Geneva Conventions laws: Oh Yes, the chemicals used by member states like white phosphorus which are banned under the convention. Protection of woman and children yet many have been trafficked and abducted.
- Refugees: Providing safety, food and shelter before returning back to their place of origin! This is very sad that people who are looking for help from a traumatic experience are turned away or exploited more.

My Story of Financial Abuse

For me, I am most certainly not money focused, and have always seen it as the root of evil; however I am learning to change my attitude towards it and see that money can help communities and enrich lives.

My money aversion actually saved me from being trafficked when I was younger, as I was not hooked on getting rich. Many perpetrators pray on victims desire to want more money.

I have however, needed money to pay my bills, and there have been times when I have had no money. It was not the fact I didn't have money, but what troubled me was how people abused me when I didn't have any. They use my fundamental needs against me and one person said I have to have sex with them so they can give me 10.00 for food! However I refused the offer and said I would rather starve to death. I had considered that person to be quite close to me, so this caused me emotional pain and a sense of disgust.

Financial abuse was one of the points of my life that I became broken. I fell into the manipulative traps of others, whom I trusted. I was very naive and gullible and I became a victim more than once. Sometimes the closer a person was to me; the harder it was to accept, and this is maybe one of the reasons it took me a long time for me to see it. Predators can quite happily leave me broken and walk off laughing at my expense, like they think I deserved it.

When I was eight months pregnant, and needed a carpet in my house for the new baby. I couldn't afford to pay a fitter. This was one time I asked for help, but instead of having help, I was just ridiculed because I needed support. So I ended up laying the carpet myself in the sitting room and on the stairs in which I became stuck as I had moved all the furniture to the other side of the room and I couldn't move it back with the heavy roll of carpet so I took a couple of days trying to lift the furniture over the carpet. Then I did the painting and drilling for the baby gates, to make sure the house was ready. I was able to complete this myself without having to be degraded myself anymore by asking for help.

Years previously, when my Italian boyfriend spoke about us getting a flat, I was flattered, as I could only afford a tiny bedsit. However, in hindsight he would not have been able to afford it without me either. He preyed on my vulnerability to have as much control over me as he could. The money wasn't split with wages being pooled, but we split all the bills down the middle even though my wages were a lot less. I would use all my wages and have nothing over and he always had money to himself. The only time he used his money on me was after he had punched me or buying me clothes, which he liked. I had no money to get out of that relationship. We had a nice flat and good food and I became dependent upon him. When I did finally leave him seven years later I had no money and a bag of clothes. My fear of destitution became less than being beaten, so I moved into a bedsit and paid 30.00 at the end of the week and no deposit.

These days, most rentals want a deposit. This keeps victims trapped in abusive situations.

There are little safety nets for victims caught in this situation. Many people have been trapped for years, suffering all forms of domestic servitude and not fulfilling their true potential. People don't choose to be a victim but often they have been beaten physically, verbally or mentally into submission. People don't just wake up as say "oh I am going to be poor". People don't wake up and say, 'I am going to be trapped for years and lose dignity, but, often it's a process that happens over a period of time under certain oppressive conditions.

Predators are often masterminds at manipulation. Whatever these predator's desire, they will obtain it. If they have negativity or jealousy towards their victim, then often they take great pleasure in destroying the victim's self-worth, in a very subtle way, just because they can. At worst, it's like a game of sadistic control, where they can then flaunt their gain as if what they have done is a premeditated trap.

I worked in the leisure industry, on minimum wage; as I hadn't any qualifications to get a higher wage, but I could work many hours as I didn't have dependants at that time. I saved up and took driving lessons and saved for a car. I never had a lot of free time. I would sleep from exhaustion but I knew if I could drive I would have more freedoms. Someone I thought highly of said her boyfriend had a car for sale and convinced me that it was a good buy, so naturally, I bought it. I was told he wanted £850, and I gave her £500 to give to him. Every month, repairs were costing over £400, which meant I had no money left over to pay for the car. She demanded the rest of the money, and then threatened me if I didn't pay it, I would be beaten up. So I drove there to explain and apologies to him for not paying the full amount yet. He explained I paid months ago, and then he asked, 'How much is she charging you?' I said the amount and he gave me a lopsided grin and, with a snarl, and he told me he only asked for £500 because the car had sat there for years, and there were a few problems. She had lied to me and her boyfriend. I had trusted her, and she had taken full advantage of me for her own gain.

After the financial abuses that I had endured, I can now reflect and see that I was far too trusting and this might be due to my asperges.

So for me personally I had become accustomed to this toxic behavior, from predators. I didn't know any different until I did my; journal, psychology and law courses, when I saw my situation as an observer. Learning the laws gave understanding of my own rights and who disrespected me and the law. I did stop contact with everyone whilst doing my journal and learnt about boundaries and implemented them. Straight away I could see those who over stepped the mark. If your elderly or very young then this is more important for you to establish a relationship with a safeguarding officer. If you're being violated then this can go to court.

What is not a supportive action, is when a vulnerable person is not getting the support they need. Their rights are breached and then they can be potentially exploited or abused, as this behavior can go under the radar. The government do have the responsibility to implement human rights and equality Acts.

'He heals the broken-hearted and binds up their wounds' (Palms 147:3) is very pertinent to this chapter.

Chapter 8

Safeguarding and Responsibilities

Safeguarding is the name given to a service used to protect any vulnerable person of any age, from abuse and exploitation. The safeguarding service is something that is put in place within schools, and care establishments. Safeguarding officers are known as key persons, and can be contacted via police stations or the council. It is important to explain to children or any vulnerable persons, where to go, and who the key person is. This can give a vulnerable person more power to obtain support if they feel they need this. This should provide any vulnerable person with a safe place and person, if needed.

All people who work within schools or children's services are required to understand the safeguarding protocol and to forward any vulnerable person through the correct channels for them to have access to support. Not every teacher is trained in safeguarding, and this is why a teacher must follow the protocol.

Reports from the National Crime Agency have revealed that gangs groom the most vulnerable in society: elderly people, single mothers, disabled people, those with mental health issues, and drug addicts. They make promises of status and wealth and then take over the victim's household (which is known as cuckooing) and operate out of the victim's homes as a base. The perpetrators often use the victim (mules) to do drug errands, and once they gain control over the victim through drugs, debt, or relationships, the domestic, sexual, violent abuses intensify, even without the perpetrator leaving the cuckooing house.

Thousands of children are being groomed (trained or conditioned), and many of these children come from broken homes, had traumatic lives, been in state care, or have been reported missing, says the NCA. Several police forces have found that children's care homes were targeted for recruiting vulnerable children; and girls were often coerced into relationships. Gangs then exploited the girls sexually and pimped them into taking, and dealing in drugs. Young girls are pimped to settle their debts. The Children's Society has called for better education to alert potential victims to the risks of becoming involved. Chief executive Matthew Reed said the report 'sheds light on the shocking scale of child grooming and exploitation by criminal gangs'.

The Children Act 1989 gave every child the right to protection, from abuse and exploitation. After this law was formed, it was then modified in 2004. Children's homes and special needs and elderly care homes have all come under scrutiny of late, and many were closed due to some form of abuse. Caroline Abrahams said it was 'deeply distressing' that the system has failed to treat them with dignity and respect or protect them from abuse and neglect. However, the report of Action on Elder Abuse revealed the abuse has been going on in their homes, perpetrated by family members. Over the twelve months, the charity received 8,961 calls; 39 per cent was for financial crime, and 33 per cent was for psychological crime. The remainder was for neglect and sexual or physical abuse.

Children's care homes have come under scrutiny for major failings; an ITV film company went undercover to film privately owned residential children's homes. The reporter managed to secure a job within the homes of the largest UK state provider group. The state provider runs more than 160 homes across the UK. The footage is shocking: public humiliation, use of restraints, children escaping on the roof, etc. There were 8,000 children living in these residential homes. Many of these children have been placed in these homes since early childhood after suffering neglect or abuse. These children have been removed from their family home due to the state definition of neglect (their parents not having enough money to feed the children), only to be put in another perilous situation.

In the previous report, families who had their benefits cut were unable to afford food and were deemed to be neglecting the children's needs, so children were placed in care. This begs the question, if the government provided adequate means and housing, for families, would they even be placed in care? Which costs taxpayers six times the amount to keep them in care, why not pay that to the parents weekly?

Children being removed from their parents—it causes long-term trauma and PTSD, American medical Journal. The psychological impact on these children for being taken away from their parents is also catastrophic. The USA Harvard report said, 'This detachment creates PTSD when a child is older.' So this method of putting children in homes is detrimental to the children development and will have further mental health implications. It is more costly to the taxpayer when the government could just give the money to the parents so that they will not be neglected to start with.

Any person who is vulnerable, often predators will seek them out and exploit them. Perpetrators make a beeline for the vulnerable, and they befriend them. Safeguarding laws have been devised to help protect any person from becoming prey.

One example of a law that is meant to help protect vulnerable people is the Care Act of 2014, which was put in place to safeguard vulnerable adults. The rules have been set out to protect people from abuse or neglect, but I am failing to see how they are protecting the vulnerable when there are so many homeless people. Homeless people are more prone to abuse and have no defenses against abuses. Quite often, they have nowhere to turn. Crisis.org.uk says more than one in three homeless people have been physically kicked or hit or suffered another form of violence whilst homeless. One in ten has been urinated on. One in twenty have been sexually attacked or assaulted whilst homeless. Almost 50 per cent have been intimidated with violence.

In 2010, David Cameron was piloting a program to help troubled families, and the government recognized a pattern of behavior for some of the people in jail. The majority of the people who were using drug rehabilitation centers came from a troubled background. These families in particular had little support; and they struggled to understand the legal system. Though the government recognized the problem, the government solution was to provide a caseworker to take notes and help the families through the bureaucratic system and through the maze of agencies with plans of getting the children to school on time. The program was set to help 120,000 families at the expense of taxpayer's money. The families felt this help was not what they needed. The bureaucratic system shouldn't be so challenging in the first place and should be accessible to all British people, but they said people don't understood this system except the civil servants who were trained. They said that if the system is accessible for all families, then a caseworker is not needed. It was a waste of taxpayers' money. The families highlighted they need psychological support, as the majority of the families had experienced abuse and needed help with trauma. The government only wanted to provide a caseworker for the system, so the people who were saying what they needed didn't have their needs met.

Legal Cases

The court may require the perpetrator to give the victim a formal apology, which can help allow the victim to gain back some control. An apology can help victims to begin the healing process and take back some control after being violated. After winning the case, a victim may feel a sense of justice, but the impact of the abuse often continues to plague a person for many years.

Victims matter. It is important that survivors stand up and exercise their rights. If they don't speak up, they can become emotionally silenced, and all forms of suppression will manifest. This is why abuse cases often surface after the perpetrator dies, because it releases the suppression.

The Negatives in the Legal Framework

Unfortunately, not all legal cases favor the victim. Some victims have not even gone to court at all. In the USA, the grand jury found several instances in which law enforcement and prosecutors failed to pursue allegations of child sexual abuse within the church. Other cases of pedophiles and rapists in the UK have not gone to court. Hearings were never sought by the police even after statements were made. This prolongs a victim mentality and is disempowering for a victim.

Without a shadow of a doubt, there are many innocent people jailed, or punitive measures applied for petty crimes, and I have seen pedophile cases get short sentences.

- There was a case only this week where a drunken lady was holding a knife inciting violence but not actually harming anyone was jailed.
- There are other vindictive cases where a person says they have been raped where the person rejected them, and are jailed.
- Persons with special needs, has been used as a scapegoat and they end up in jail to protect the real perpetrator.

There have been some very unethical decisions by judges where the decision has been overturned also.

In the UK, the most senior police officer once said pedophiles who view indecent images should not be given criminal sanctions unless they pose a physical threat to children. This belief is likely, due to saturation levels which have emerged from recent findings.

The cost of solicitors is not supportive to many victims or people, including people with learning needs or disabilities. Many people being controlled have little access to funds, hence the abuse. If the perpetrator holds the finance then they are in a better position to get a better lawyer which discriminates against the poorer person who is potentially a victim and feels ashamed so this keeps a person silenced, and have lesser legal representation. Victims should be able to have the best lawyer and have the same advantage as the controlling partner.

Many survivors don't feel that the law supports survivors or victims enough. Justice shouldn't be defaulted to financial means. It is not deemed fair, and most victims, by their nature of being a victim, don't have the means to fight. This is how so many perpetrators get away with monstrosities. There are law firms who work on a 'no win, no fee' basis.

In some geographic regions, many women who have been victims of trafficking have ended up with criminal records, so not only have they have been exploited by their perpetrator; they have then been penalized by the legal system, this law has however started to change in many countries however this also depends upon the judge.

Family courts have come under scrutiny in the last few years, as for systematic failings to consider 'injunctions'. Violent or controlling partners have been allowed to sit in close proximity and intimidate their ex-partner as this has more serious legal implications.

Women's Aid	0808-2000-247
NSPCC	0808-800-5000
Samaritans	08457-90-90-90
Childline	0800-1111
Refuge	0808-2000-247
Anxiety	08444-775-774
Victim Support	0845-30-30-900
Family Lives	0808-800-2222

Reporting Abuse

Reporting the abuse for me was a daunting task; as this had chewed me up emotionally for years. I found it hard to process my thoughts and talking about it, was even harder. I was never encouraged to speak up and I didn't want to be known as a troublemaker. By not reporting the abuse, kept me in a victims state of mind. I spent years deliberating if I should report it, and I felt more like a coward for not reporting it. The stiff upper lip attitude that us British have is not always supportive. However the traumas were affecting my life, and the perpetrators were getting away with it and potentially abusing others.

I almost backed out when I was in the police station. I was also hoping that if I report it, I would feel an emotional release but I actually felt so bad and disgusted with myself. It was then; I had to accept what happened and take responsibility and not live in denial. I had to face these toxic memories that sat in my mind, tormenting me for years, and affecting many aspects of my life. And here I was in the police station striking back at the perpetrator and not allowing them to get away with it anymore. I finally reported the child abuse and rape in my thirties.

The Child abuse:

Time passed by after I reported it and I hadn't heard a thing, and I had to pluck up more courage to called them, a year later. A policewoman was sent to my house and took my statements again. I had to regurgitate it all a second time. I asked about the previous notes, and she just explained she would take them now to investigate it, and said she didn't have enough information to follow up the rape case. They followed up the child abuse and went to his house, and he apparently denied it. The policewoman said he was very poorly and that he probably wouldn't last that long. I wasn't asked if I want to take it to court and I was a little shocked after I took years to actually report it that nothing happened, he just walked away.

The Rape:

Years passed by and when I was doing my degree, I became an emotional wreck with the Jimmy Savile pedophile case. My triggers were going off and were creating massive anxiety, depression, and panic attacks for me daily. The crime-stoppers provided a helpline number for those affected by this, which I phoned in confidence. I explained what happened and they investigated the rape, even though the policewoman previously said they had little information and couldn't investigate it. Scotland Yard took it more seriously and followed the few leads. They located the house, his ex wife and confirmed dates and everything.

They said I was fifteen almost sixteen when I was raped, as of the timeline which made me technically a child, and told me the rapist died of a heart attack a few months after he raped me. The rapist's ex-wife suspected this and her son. The police provided me with all the facts, and I received a verbal apology from the police and from my abuser's ex-wife. It was incredibly strange to finally feel the relief that came from hearing the apology—even though it wasn't directly from my abuser. The rapist's ex-wife commented at how evil he was. The relief that I had with the apology gave me closure. It took away my self-blame and the guilt. I could finally forgive myself. It made me feel less of a coward and less of a victim for speaking out. This gave me closure. I could accept that I was not to blame and that it was he who held all responsibility for taking advantage of me.

CHAPTER 9

Impact on Survivors

Me at the model of the year beauty pageant 2017
before winning Classic Model UK

If victims do not get support, their mental health suffers. Many doctors can't assess a patient at face value, as there is often no physical evidence noticeable. It is a challenge for victims to talk about their abuses or trauma, and many victims don't associate this with mental health but wellbeing. Mental health stigma has put many people off seeking professional help. Mental health is so diverse however, and even though the victim doesn't have neurological disorders, Stress, Depression, Anxiety, Eating Disorders, PTSD does fall under mental health.

Post-traumatic stress syndrome or disorder, caused by a very stressful state of awareness, often stemmed from a perceived life threatening event that had occurred. PTSD can inhibit natural freedoms that a person experienced before the event/abuse happened.

An example: If the victim experienced a catastrophe at sea, then the victim may develop an aversion or fear assimilated to the sea. The life-threatening experience often creates an adverse reaction for the victim. As a survivor becomes closer to the repeated stimulus (sea) it can cause a surge of fear that can be overwhelming or overpowering to a survivor. This fear can often dominate a person and prevent them from going near the sea, inhibiting freedoms.

A trigger/stimulus: is the cause that created a reaction: i.e, comedy can be the trigger to laughter (cause and effect) If the trigger causes fear, (as in the example of the sea), the person can react in an adverse way. This is because of the previous experiences which compromised the person's safety. This is perfectly rational. A phobia is irrational and often has no point of origin.

Reaction: As the fear is induced this causes a reaction: fight, flight, or freeze is experienced by the survivor. This reaction (Fight, flight, or freeze) contributes to how the survivor responds to the fear. If the person reaction is to fight, then they may become angry and want to hit something. If the reaction to the fear is flight then they may run away and avoid the situation. Other survivors may just freeze and become numb to any suggestion.

Coping Strategies: After responding to fear stimulus a person can feel overwhelmed, and they often look at ways to calm down, like singing etc. This is known as coping strategies. They can be behavior or thought patterns to reduce stress and anxiety- There are many different strategies, which will help people to reduce stress and allow a person to cope.

<u>Denial</u>: Is a coping mechanism that gives a person mental space to adjust to an uncomfortable situation. However denial can hinder a person from accepting the truth or abuse.

<u>Defense Mechanism</u>: Is often denial, forgetting, rationalizing, and repression. Repression is the fundamental defense mechanism in Freudian theory- what you forget can't hurt you.

<u>Habits:</u> This habitual behavior is a repetitive pattern of behavior. This can become the norm, and a part of the person's way of life. Coping strategies can become a habit. Some habits can become a limitation and leant upon as a crutch. It's sometimes just as painful to remove the habit as it is to deal with the trauma. You can identify what your coping strategies are when you do a journal.

Mental health problems can manifest for years before the survivor even knows anything is wrong, as survivors develop coping strategies that become habitual. This habit can be identified when the survivor keeps a journal. Unfortunately, some strategies are unhealthy and more damaging in the long term to the body like alcoholism, drug abuse, or smoking; and the victim may become dependent upon them. In this situation, the victim not only has to break an addiction but also has to identify that their addiction is attached to a previous trauma.

If the trauma is very painful, then the conscious memory can block it out(defense mechanism, denial) Sometimes the only way to access these memories of trauma is through hypnosis by a trained psychologist. There is no guarantee that these painful memories can be recalled until the person feels safe and is ready to deal with them. There is no measure of time. Painful memories can still be triggered by a similar stimuli, the memory still retains associated links to the event, like a smell, taste, touch and the person may of built an aversion to this, and can induce unexplained anxiety or negative feelings..

<u>Limiting beliefs:</u> These beliefs are often indoctrinated by other people's opinions, it is what other people have potentially said and a survivor has not challenged this. If it not encouraging words then it could be constraining which is often a artificial benchmark set by another person so the survivor doesn't think they are able to go above this benchmark.

<u>Stockholm syndrome</u> is more common than what is realized, this is mostly associated with kidnapping and abductions, where a victim bonds with a perpetrator. A part of the victim needs to understand why would they do that? It's a form of rationalizing..

Remember it's never the victims fault.

The Brain Function

Stress is governed by two bodily responses through the endocrine system, hormonal response, and neurological response via the chemical messengers.

If the stress hormone damages the hippocampus (in the brain) due to excessive Cortisol then memory retention can be compromised and a person can suffer from memory loss.

In a war situation, comrades fight together against what's known as the enemy. Soldiers are trained to fight and learn how to use ammunition. They are not fully taught about the mental processes. The mental training is about defending and attacking, to protect their country. Both sides try to protect themselves and their countries, when their platoon gets injured then fear is elevated, and a natural chemical reaction in the brain is released. Fear is often stoked by the stress hormone (Cortisol), which keeps soldiers at the ready for extended periods of time.

Excess Cortisol creates havoc on the mind and body. This is one of the stress hormones responsible for the fight, flight, or freeze response, along with adrenaline. Adrenaline and Cortisol are responsible for that immediate reaction that gives the person or animal the surge of power needed to run away from a dangerous situation. It also creates laser-sharp focus. This is a natural survival mechanism within the bodies of animals and humans. Some soldiers try to evade war and maybe it's their elevated Cortisol which created the flight response which is instinctive. Some soldiers may have the freeze response and are not able to pull the trigger. The Cortisol hormone is not just in soldiers but is also in any person who is experiencing a heightened level of fear. If fear doesn't subside, the stress hormones will continue to flood the body and create a reactive state.

When people suffer from PTSD, it is the initial trigger that activates the hormones from the endocrine system, if the fear is not removed the body will start to produce excessive Cortisol.

And when the body is constantly in stress, the brain has a difficult time getting the body to respond correctly. In the case of soldiers, the fear and Cortisol make them ever ready for combat. Unfortunately, continued elevated levels of Cortisol can cause damage and brings about mental illness.

Cortisol is produced by the adrenal glands. When the levels of Cortisol are elevated (due to stress), it can also cause high blood pressure, high blood sugar, and low bone density. Cortisol can also suppress the immune system, decrease libido, produce acne, and contribute to obesity. A little amount of stress is good in order to focus, but too much of it is detrimental. Other symptoms can include irregular heartbeat and sweating—which is why when people have PTSD flashbacks, they break out in a sweat. That is the result of the adrenaline hormone surge prior to the Cortisol surge. If there has been too much Cortisol over a period of time then the person is likely to depression, and sexual dysfunction or low libido.

The amygdala in the brain recognizes the threat (e.g. a gun being pointed at you). This action sends signals around the body's neurological system and shuts the brain down, so it goes into survival mode, allowing action without or before thinking. The body has dropped into a reactive state and is ready for action with the sympathetic nervous system, which controls involuntary actions. Hormones are released in a domino effect from the hypothalamus, then the pituitary gland, and then the adrenal gland, which then produces Cortisol.

These stress hormones have nothing to do with reproductive hormones, which are progesterone, oestrogen, and the testosterone.

Neurotransmitters (the brain's communicator) can influence the neuron—directly or indirectly affecting behavior. The four main neurotransmitters that regulate the mood are:

Norepinephrine is a hormone and neurotransmitter for anti-stress reaction. It increases the heart rate and triggers the release of glucose for conversion to energy. It helps with blood flow to muscles and reduces blood to the gastrointestinal system. The sympathetic nervous system's response triggers the adrenaline response, and Cortisol. It works in conjunction with other hormones and neurotransmitters. Too much is linked to anxiety and hyperactivity and too little can cause lethargy, inattention, and lack of focus or concentration.

1. Dopamine is the feel-good neurotransmitter found in pleasurable activities and food. High amounts of dopamine can also cause euphoria, aggression, and intense sexual feelings. Too low dopamine can lead to too-low motivation, fatigue, weight gain, low libido, depression, ADHD, binge eating, Alzheimer's, Parkinson's, bipolar disorder, addiction, and schizophrenia.

2. The GABA neurotransmitter is meant to reduce or calm the central nervous system (CNS). It is used for relieving pain (e.g. PMS),

promoting lean muscle, and burning fat. High amounts lead to anxiousness, feeling edgy, insomnia, and a fearful attitude. Too little causes less muscle tone, leading to muscle stiffness or hyper tonicity.

3. Serotonin helps regulate mood. Lack of sunlight can cause low serotonin. High amounts of serotonin can cause shivering, diarrhea, and seizures. Low amounts can cause neurotransmitter imbalances, memory loss, loss of appetite, and poor mood.

Neurotransmitters exchange chemicals to inhibit or facilitate the fine equilibrium towards the healthy brain and body. If the transmitters have the correct balance, then the person will function well. If the person is under stress, the stress hormones override thinking, and survival behavior overrule any rationality. We know from earlier findings that sustained elevated Cortisol hinders thinking and is responsible for depression via the endocrine system. SSRI antidepressants work with neurotransmitters and not the endocrine system against elevated Cortisol, so antidepressants are often ineffective in those who have a lot of stress. SSRI will still continue to work by inhibiting feelings, but the Cortisol will make a person behave irrationally.

A study at the 168th annual meeting of the American Psychiatric Association (APA) showed that patients with elevated salivary Cortisol levels failed to respond to treatment with selective serotonin reuptake inhibitor Fluoxetine (Prozac, Sarafem). Prozac was an antidepressant; Sarafem is marketed to women as a treatment for premenstrual syndrome. Earlier studies have linked poor responses to other types of antidepressants in people with high Cortisol levels. According to Liver Doctor (www.liverdoctor.com), if you have elevated Cortisol levels, then antidepressants are less likely to work.

An interesting study is on how dopamine can reduce the levels of Cortisol. Dopamine can be found in avocados, bananas, almonds, lima beans, pumpkin seeds, and sesame seeds. Fruit and vegetables help protect dopamine using neurons. Oxytocin is also an inhibitor or reducer of Cortisol. Oxytocin is the chemical produced by hugging, kissing, sex, and orgasm and is known as the love hormone or the bonding hormone. This releases the antidote to depression.

Cortisol has a similar effect on animals as it does on humans. Stress degrades the body's immune system, and some animals experience excessive thirst, irregular heart rate, low blood sugar, low potassium, tremors, gastrointestinal issues affecting weight, and low libido. In humans, cortisol is also responsible for the blood sugar, weight gain around the abdomen, sleep issues, low sex drive, and disrupted reproductive cycles. The reaction also moves the blood away from the abdomen.

When a person is in a deep sleep, the unconscious mind is often in theta state. Dreams or nightmares evolve from the subconscious memory. (flashbacks) This memory has a lot to process. If a person experienced a horrific trauma but can't access all the memories due to coping mechanisms, then these memories can be accessed by hypnosis in the alpha state, where a trained hypnotherapist can gain access to that memory as the patient or survivor recalls the memory subconsciously. In beta state, which is when a person is awake and conscious, they may not be able to recall the memories due to denial and pain associated with the event. Stress, which induces Cortisol, also inhibits the memory.

It can be traumatic to reiterate the ordeal, and the survivor may have heightened awareness as the stress hormones surge around the body and brain. This can cause trouble in trying to sleep or rest. The resistance of the alpha state helps a person to stay in control, or fight sleep, but when they finally get to sleep, they may have trouble waking up. The surge in stress hormones can also have a negative effect and make the victim very tired, needing to sleep in order to reduce Cortisol or use sleep as a stress release.

How Are You Feeling?

Sutton Trust's findings: child trauma thinking will deviate to coping instead of long term ambitious goals. Abuse at any age will have an effect on a person's health and well-being.

Despite the pain and suffering the survivor experiences during and after the abuse, there are many therapies that can support survivors to push through the barriers and learn to fully embrace life again. It is not easy, and the therapies can take many months, if not years, to work through. Ask your doctor for a list of therapy courses you can go on. It is often the patient who has to ask the doctor for a particular therapy. Many GPs and doctors are often not trained in mental health, so this is why you need to be specific so that they can help. All survivors deserve to live life to the fullest, and after you work through some of the trauma, you will have a new lease of life. Hopefully, my book will be your turning point to your healing.

Trigger Impact on Me

Child Abuse: When I was at school, in a sex education lesson, I comprehended what had previously happened to me (child sexual abuse) by my neighbor. I was sat in school feeling so sick and numb when I understood what he had done; I felt awkward at the time of the abuse but as my parents were naturist I just thought it was normal to walk around with your private parts out. I didn't realize his actions with his private parts were wrong either, so this had really taken advantage of my innocence. When I walked home from school, and approached my home, I felt terrified. I tried to pretend I was fine. I was shaking and then I blanked him and his house. I climbed through our toilet window into my house. My reaction to this fear was denial; the triggers cause me to emotionally shut down. My triggers were not just that man, but it was: a numerous aspects associated with that abuse like, having to go to nudist beaches and see men's penis, milk, certain dogs, etc and these all became associated triggers. When I came into contact with these trigger it heightened my fear.

Child abuse: I was sexually attacked when I was 13, in a bus, by the conductor, I froze, and when he opened the door I bolted out, and ran. My reaction to the trigger was I was frozen then flight. I have never been able to go on a bus by myself since this. I would walk everywhere to avoid catching a bus.

Not all my reactions have been so calm. I have asperges and I need to keep my surroundings organized to function or I get flustered. My stress increases, and the only way to reduce this stress- is to tidy. My initial reaction to this trigger is often calm as I am processing the information, and then I react, i.e, I tidy. However, if I can't tidy up, my stress level continues to increase.

In this case: I had a friend who came around and sat on the floor and not the settee, he put his carrier bags all over the floor and settee. That irritated me and I asked him to put them in the corner, which he didn't. I was hospitable and made him a cup of tea, but the mess was irritating me. I could feel my body getting tense, causing panic, so I asked him to leave my house, but he refused. I ended up throwing cups and plates at him. I reacted in fight mode. However, initially my mind was processing my thoughts, until it became so overwhelming for me. This is overwhelm is also known as a meltdown. This is where my emotions are controlling me, and not I am in control. If items are not in the correct place then this does affect myself and many other people who suffer with autism.

Raped: When I was being raped at 15, my reaction was freeze initially, and I couldn't move or speak, but after a while I managed to shout. My stressed level climbed so high that it made me react.

My triggers associated with this trauma were: dress with popper buttons, round tables, and tiny windows, heights, feeling trapped or enclosed. If I experience any of these then my fear level increases dramatically.

Analyzing my own reactions to fear:

The fear was so bad that, even as I think about it, I can feel my brain shutting down. I have tried to analysis my reactions, and thoughts to fear, so I have greater awareness of what is happening to me. It's very hard to control thoughts under the conditions of fear. When my fear is heightened, it feels like everything is in slow motion. On reflection it seemed like I was not present, but I was observing- like I was watching a film but not in the film. If you asked me a question in this state of mind, then I don't know if I could answer. My brain controlled my body, and the longer I was in this stressed state of mind, my body felt more numb. My reasoning was becoming void, whilst my reaction was building. I was able to observe but not respond initially.

Even though the actual event or abuse leaves a psychological impact, so do the inanimate objects surrounding the event, which are often future triggers. Now, as a result of what has happened to me I try to avoid triggers, I could not afford a psychiatrist or psychologist but I was diagnosed with PTSD at my local hospital by a nurse who worked for the psychiatrist but nothing was ever recommended other than putting myself on a waiting list for a counselor. Talk therapy over 6 weeks and you have to reapply, for me I couldn't even talk about any of these abuses in that time. So if you are like me, you need to take the bull by the horns and look at finding techniques and ways to help yourself. This book will highlight some or the ones that helped me. These traumatic memories never leave, but you can lessen the impact it has on you. Processing your feelings, thoughts and behavior to different stimulus can help to de-sensitize you. Gain a better understanding of how the abuse affected you personally and how you can change your perception in many ways, and use forgiveness.

You can improve your life, and become more aware of how your external world has affected your internal behavior. Cognitive behavior is extremely good for helping you to understand this. However you need to learn to be kind to yourself because if you don't respect yourself then you will not necessarily know when others are disrespecting you.

Don't blame yourself for other people's actions or hidden agenda, we are all unique and if someone abuses you, then it violates you as again they do not know your boundaries or other peoples boundaries. They often abuse their position of power and disrespect other people in many ways.

When you work through the traumas then pat yourself on the back but don't take it for granted that you are cured. It takes a while to heal but when it affects you less then you are most certainly on the right path.

CHAPTER 10

Healing

Healing is about overcoming obstacles—whether they're limiting beliefs, self-imposed limitations, anxiety, fears etc. Even the smallest steps you can take will help you overcome inner negativity. Observing your own behaviors can help in supporting your personal development. Practicing or gaining the knowledge being in the moment and safe will assist you in your healing when your memories become overwhelming. Reflecting on the past through journaling can help a person ascertain where and how the: limiting beliefs, coping strategies, triggers etc have evolved and how they have affected one's behavior. You can also learn how to change this so the trauma and triggers has a lesser affect on the person. The objective of overcoming traumatic pressures is to eliminate some of the barriers that impede your freedoms.

- Anxiety- This is often a feeling of unease, worry or fear. This is from the central nervous system and long term anxiety can cause your brain to release the stress hormone Cortisol. After the release of Cortisol then the body's by product creates depression.
- Behaviors-The way a person conducts themselves and expresses themselves
- Clinical depression – is a deeper and extended depression.
- Confidence-When a person has confidence then they know they are capable of a task, or can be reliable etc. Whenever you start something new you probably won't know much about it,

hence it is new. So don't allow others to put you off because you don't know a lot. You're not meant to know a lot or it's not new. Confidence comes with practice or repetition. When you feel happy doing something, then you know you've got it. However some people take longer to get it than others. How to walk with confidence? When a person feels they've got it then they feel proud and quite often the posture changes. Again, if you take any person out of their comfort area into a new area they will have to learn a new skill or adapt. Confidence will need to be learnt again.

- Depression- This low feeling or mood means a person can lose interest in activities they often enjoy. Negative feelings are associated with this: guilt, low self worth, with some unhealthy behaviors as: disturbed sleep, low appetite, poor concentration.
- Post traumatic Stress Disorder- An after effect of a trauma
- Self esteem- Quite often, teachers, parents or a boss at work, place high expectations on you, and if you have low self esteem, you may experience self-doubt. The defensive feeling maybe felt and expressed through; anger, blame, control, neglect, compulsive behavior, fear, hurt, or perfectionism. Expectations are often not encouraging. Objectives are goals, if they are set too high, this can be perceived to be unobtainable and can often belittle or tear a person down. To build self esteem means accepting yourself as you are, be authentic and start listening to your own needs, and not be hard on yourself. You need to know your worth and not let others limit you. The negative emotions often stem from what other people have projected onto you ; which can limit your beliefs. If you allow people to limit your beliefs then this can damage your self-esteem. This can make a person feel worthless. These self-imposed limiting beliefs can hold a person back from becoming his or her true, authentic self.
- Trauma-An event or situation that can cause overwhelm and excessive stress overload.

Below are some methods and therapies that can support your development. If you are still in an adverse situation, it isn't advisable for you to start a journal. Doing so could potentially compromise your safety. You need to be in a safe environment before you begin, and I encourage you to use the resources listed throughout the book.

Some therapies to support you through encouraging the expression of feelings and emotions:

- Laughter as healing helps with low mood.
- Play therapy helps to express feelings.
- Art therapy helps to express feelings.
- Music therapy helps to express emotions.
- Dancing therapy helps to express body language and feelings or emotions.
- Shopping helps to boost well-being, confidence, self-worth.
- CBT helps in many ways.
- NLP helps with confidence and making the initial step, especially good for phobias and reframing for confidence.
- Mindfulness is for anxiety and depression but is not helpful for trauma unless it is used alongside another therapy. I find this is a good way to lift you up quickly out of challenging times. As I went through my trauma with other therapies, I became so down that I needed to use mindfulness to bring me out of that previous pain in the PTSD state.
- Journals 1 and timelines are especially good for reflection and pinpointing areas where help might have been required.
- Journals 2 are for recalling painful feelings and memories or senses or facts. Use emojis as this can make it easier for the writer. The writer can go back and forth as he or she feels comfortable. Journaling in conjunction with professional therapy can help a person be able to understand where these painful memories came from and how to change them. Use this journal to process

old memories; it can help to reflect back and see things in a first-hand point of view, but then as you read over your writing, you can detach yourself slightly and look at the experience objectively, which helps to remove difficult emotions from it.

- Stretching and fitness help to alleviate anger
- Church or Bible groups and prayer are in order for you to have faith in something else. This helps with feelings of abandonment and promotes the feeling of being loved no matter who you are.
- Group work enables you to meet others who are facing similar traumas.
- Group therapy is where you join a group or watch an interactive service online.
- Eye movement de-sensitization and reprocessing (EMDR) is a proven effective treatment for trauma.
- Hypnotherapy and Bowen help with depression, phobias, etc. by addressing the subconscious mind.
- Tapping is a technique that has better results when you are working with a therapist. Tapping detracts the attention from the conscious mind and creates a direct response from the subconscious. This is often a quicker way of locating the root of the problems than other techniques. It should be followed by the NLP technique.

These therapies help with stress reduction:

- affirmations
- Reflexology (massage, spa day, etc.)
- aromatherapy massage, hot stone massage
- Arts (knitting, painting, Jewellery making, drawing, etc.)
- hypnotherapy
- praying
- being in nature (e.g. going on a picnic)
- singing and music

- exercise and dance
- mindfulness
- meditation with audio (meditating in silence can be difficult for victims of abuse and trauma; try meditating to calming music or a guided meditation audio)
- walking in safe areas
- writing (sometimes you may feel like you are at the breaking point, and writing everything down and possibly sharing them with your therapist can help you understand what it is you are feeling and can help you look at the triggers that are causing specific thoughts or emotions)
- stretching (meditation and yoga are great ways to clear the mind and focus on healing; you can meditate or perform in the quiet or whilst listening to calming music or chant positive words or affirmations)

Prehealing

Many people suffer from loneliness, anxiety, depression, traumas, etc.; and often people need to be listened to and require more help, physically, mentally, or general guidance.

If a person is alone, even the touch of a pet can help. To listen means to identify how you can really help the person! Ascertain what they really need and what they are really saying and see if you can help them, or can find someone who can help them. Maybe the housewife wants shelves put up, but the husband just says, 'Oh, she keeps on moaning!' If he were to put the shelves up or find someone else who can, then maybe she wouldn't moan about it anymore. But more than that, she needs to feel heard and validated. Having your feelings and thoughts validated does so much good to your sense of self-worth.

People need to feel valued, and not: bullied, belittled, and discriminated against, abuse, so they are cowering from who they are. These defense mechanisms that victims acquire can also prevent many positive emotions. The walls can become self-imposed limitations, so it's important to recognize these and to see if the walls are servicing you or hindering your emotional health. For example, I had a phobia of people, and I convinced myself I couldn't leave my house because people do hurtful things. I stayed in my house to protect myself. This situation limited any enjoyment I could have.

Forgiveness is a really valuable tool to support your own development.

Do not hold on to any guilt from being abused, or to any embarrassment If speaking to a therapist is too challenging, then write it down in a journal. Some heavy emotional burden can be expressed in writing, art, dance, music, etc. so they won't be trapped within the body.

Every person is different and has different capabilities, good and bad points. We are all unique; and should value this. This does not mean you should allow any abuse or threats to continue, however.

There is an eye for an eye philosophy, but a victim doesn't have to abuse another person. You can forgive and be the stronger one, you can learn to heal yourself and support people in the way you would like to be treated. You do not have to kick a person when they are down simply because you saw others do that or because other people did that to you.

Healing is an act of lessening the pain and of restoring your body and mind from negativity and finding methods to lessen the traumatic stress. This personal empowerment will help you strive to be the best version of yourself.

We all need to evolve and know we are loved. Listen to yourself to build self- esteem. Happiness comes from inside. The process of healing is not on a stopwatch. There is no rush. Be kind to yourself now and always.

Replace My Thorns with Love: My Impetus for Change

When I reached my forties, I was agoraphobic and had a fear of people. I was having frequent anxiety and panic attacks as I tried to leave my house, and my heart would feel like it was racing. This became so overwhelming that it resulted to ordering my food online. If I left my house, I would quickly return home, where I would consume a big breath of air and sigh in relief. I became so trapped and didn't see this as a mental health issue.

I was constantly exhausted and succumbed to low energy levels, but when I did sleep, I had bad dreams and flashbacks, which disorientated me. Basic tasks were a huge effort—even getting dressed.

I became a recluse, and my negativity ran so deep, I didn't understand why. Months and years passed while I was in this state. I had attempted to work over this time, but the challenge of me leaving the house all became too much and I would end up having to cancel work. Fortunately, I had a childminder up until she retired to look after my child to make sure he socialized, and enabled me to complete my degree mostly; it was a struggle for me to get to the university also, if I got there at all so I completed this at home.

I started to analyze my thoughts and my situation, and I had no one to turn to. I just craved love, but when I had a child minder up until she retired to who said they loved me I still felt empty, it was fruitless so I would turn to sleep as my coping strategy. I felt safer if I slept. I could close the world out and hide away.

Hiding away was not really an answer long-term though and this was the issue. I consulted a counselor and she asked, "do I felt suicidal" I thought that was such a dumb question. I had felt suicidal most of my life, but I wasn't going to hurt myself because the very thought of actually hurting myself made me wince. Of course, I felt suicidal. When I was at my weakest, I was easy prey, so I was hardly likely to tell a person I didn't know, trained or not, that I felt that way. I did not trust any person. She suggested I do education courses, so I accepted this. Over time, I did some courses on psychology and watched the Online Church, which was educational and healing. I felt safe as I was in my own environment and I could listen to the Word, which I found very supportive. Crying released the pain. The church was always profoundly effective. I enjoyed learning; I also looked at YouTube videos on building my confidence. I found all the different subjects I was learning about to be empowering.

I analyzed my feelings and noticed inadequacies, and questioned "why I felt so low". I had been through so much that I didn't know where to start. I started with what made me happy and that was the church. So I would listen to the church, and isolate what made me feel good and what made me feel bad. This was not so easy as I had experiences and thoughts which had a negative impact on me, and positive ones. So I decided to isolate these and look at what makes me feel this. This was the start of my journal.

As I processed my thoughts I would type, anything that just popped up that caused me an issue I would put that down too. I noticed silly things like I felt guilty for feeling happy! I then questioned this! Why? A lot of painful truths and abuses surfaced, memories that I had totally forgotten came to the surface too. I had very low self worth, no self esteem or confidence and I didn't really know much about myself. I knew I was creative and arty, I had spent my life being a people pleaser and supporting others.

So I researched how to resolve my issues, and I had a couple of inspiring friends, or none judgmental people that spoke kind supportive words. The pastor friend told me not to accept these things people are telling me about me, because it's a lie. I had always listened to everyone else's opinions. In hindsight I can't believe I based my worth on what others said, but I did.

The Pastor was very good as he knew the heartache and trauma I had faced and he said that God is my constant, and he has always loved me and that's all I need. I loved this, because I had felt abandoned and knowing this made me feel complete and not needy anymore. I decided that I only need God and good people around me so I decided to stop contacting everyone, my asperges couldn't let me discern between good people and toxic people so I stopped all contact.

Not phoning people was strange at first but I resisted, I decided to clear any toxic person out of my life, it was good to see who enquired about me (3 persons) and who never called again (everyone else). Many of these people undermined, belittled, and bullied me. However at the time I didn't see it like that. I loved them and couldn't understand why anyone would want to deliberately lie and hurt me.

The pastor said all my negative beliefs came from what others had said and not the truth. Then I came to the conclusion that I didn't even know much about myself; I only knew what others had told me about me, and then I realized that God was my only constant. My solitude became my respite, where I could recharge my batteries and sit alone in contemplation and pray.

I was incredibly in denial, about my feeling, my needs and also my rights, people just walked all over me, and I had allowed them because I hadn't known any different. I had faced abuse upon abuse, and never really dealt with it or how this had even affected me.

There seemed to be little help for this, I had spoken to my doctor and was forwarded to a councilor but that was a little superficial, and I never even spoke about most of the abuses.

In my learning I became aware of NLP. Tim Tarango gave me a lot of advice with Neuro -linguistic programming in which is used for : confidence, changing negativity and sales, for reaching the ceiling. This metaphor was actually my physical ceiling- and this helped me to push beyond my limits, and leave my house without anxiety. I worked on this everyday for over three months. It was so exciting to be able to take steps towards my freedom. I embraced this learning and took on board many other programs and techniques and implemented the lot.

I decided I was making progress, and decided I had been held back by my limiting beliefs,(lack of confidence, self-esteem etc) so pushed myself through my comfort zone I took my GCSE that I was unable to do at 16 due to my circumstances, this was tougher than my degree, mentally. But I knew I had God, and he was holding me up, metaphorically speaking. As I was progressing with this positivity and moving forward, I started to work through PTSD. My journal was starting to build of all the events and times of the abuses to give me a clearer picture of what was still affecting me, there were so many things affecting my life and so many unresolved issues, and my emotions were up and down as I was working through this.

I constantly reflected back to when I was 15 and to the life I had, and all the traumas from that time. It was very tough though.

So I would reflect back on my notes from my journal. My notes started to contain details on my coping strategy which was really useful for me to observe them, especially if I became overwhelmed by a trigger. I would be able to ascertain why that had affected me, and what my coping strategy is quickly. When my triggers goes I can't think or focus, as my body goes into fear mode- by reflecting on my journal gives me the ability to reflect and to see what I need to implement to calm me quicker. I can also use reverse psychology if I find I am repeating a habit associated to a coping strategy to isolate a potential trigger to what induce this.

I continued to learn and implement healthier behaviors, but I had to identify my habits and behaviors first. This is not easy to suddenly change a habit or behavior but when I was aware then I would watch my response, and process my thoughts before I responded.

My development was progressing and I decided to learn human rights and international law, more psychology. After 1-2 years from starting the journals and healing I was able to leave my house more after preparing myself and I was able to have a few quality days with my son and managed to go to the beach and swim in the sea; my son totally enjoyed himself and learnt to surf. I even tried camping with my son one day even though the camp site is 10 minutes away; I was still trying something different, and pushing my limits. I was absolutely freezing though and my toes were numb, but it was an adventure and my son enjoyed it.

When I pushed forward I would tackle more of the journal and reflect, I would not have been able to progress had I not had the small breakthroughs. I did have some very low points as I was working through my journal and processing the traumas and my feelings. Seeing all the denial that I had been through was becoming transparent, I could see all the abuses which I had conveniently blocked out previously. This was a shock to me as all my human rights had been breached at some point, and some people used and abused me and lied to me which led to many limiting beliefs, but knowing my rights now is empowering. The fact human rights are not widely known was actually alarming.

I took on challenges that I would never have tried before. My journal was filling up and I was forgiving more people, the church helped me to do that. I was slowly progressing. I decided to challenge my limiting beliefs, and I took a massive plunge into an area I knew nothing about because one man said I was beautiful, but previous I was led to believe by others that I was: too old, skinny legs, and a bunch of derogatory comments, so I joined a national beauty pageant and I won the second pageant after finding out what one wears to such events and won the title "Classic Model of the Year UK". Winning the pageant changed my life. I felt like I had a voice. My limited beliefs crumbled before me, and the truth was I had believed all these lies which had restrained me for so many years; I never challenged what others had said but just accepted it because that is what I was told to do. It was mentally challenging to put myself out there, and it took a massive leap of faith, this brought me closer to God, and I now know my purpose is to help others who have limiting beliefs and to support people who have experienced trauma. That is one of the main reasons I wrote this book.

Writing and Designing My Plan of Healing

The advice I can suggest is that safety is paramount. Make sure that if you are thinking of delving into your past to resolve any issues, you should be in a safe environment. Having a professional therapist or pastor for support is also recommended. The emotions that can surface can be an array of blame, self-pity, anxiety, depression, and anger, and you can feel many emotions:

- neglect
- fear
- worthlessness
- guilt
- shame
- low
- no confidence
- betrayal
- panic attacks
- violation

These are emotions that you may find yourself working through are potentially harbored unresolved emotions. The past has gone, and you are only reflecting to spot patterns but not to dwell for too long in past painful experiences. I knew the fear belonged in the past and not in the present, which is really important when reflecting back as the mind can replay the event over and over so I use mindfulness to ground myself. Mindfulness is about focusing on the here and now by feeling texture etc and being very aware of where you are now, this can bring attention to how safe you are now.

What I experienced when I started my healing journey was like taking the lid off a can of worms and letting all the worms out. So many issues that I was not expecting surfaced. What I thought was just a confidence issue turned out to be a lot more. I used the journal so I could ascertain when the traumas happened so I could establish which traumas still had a hold on me, so that I could resolve and dissipate the stronghold it had over me.

I found several root problems which pertained to elevating negative emotions. Some were worse than others, so I had to work through many issues—from being violated to being abandoned—to build my self-esteem and worth and to love and forgive myself and others and to become compassionate to myself. I knew as emotions were continuing to arise that it was going to be a long, arduous process.

I discovered how limiting beliefs led to not having self esteem; I learnt to recognize my coping strategies, and triggers. I saw the impact these had on my life; I was able to employ methods to completely turn my life around.

My Reflection Led Me to Greater Awareness

Prior to the start of my journey I was agoraphobic and needed to solve this. The request for help fell upon deaf ears, with pip and support for PTSD, however I was offered counseling for 6 hours, over the weeks.

Over the years I started to aim towards private therapy, educational techniques, international law and human rights, how the brain functions and the body under stress. I tried to look at many options to reduce stress, and to research different cases of abuses and continuing investigations.

My research led me to greater awareness and where there are pitfalls in society. How injustice is not just worn by the victims and survivors but how it affects society as a whole. There is little unity and support which weakens a society.

To create a society means looking after neighbors and the vulnerable, however the attitude, being the - "me me me" hedonistic society has made unreasonable sacrifices for more wealth. This perilous situation causes a break down in care, and interpersonal relationships. The focused upon their objective, often disregard the children, elderly, vulnerable persons where they are left to fend for themselves, and needs are not met. Although there appears to be safety nets to protect the vulnerable (PIP) (care homes) these are often ineffective at best, or worst case do more harm than good, especially when they become political footballs. This often leads to gross exploitation and potentially abuse to those most vulnerable.

So many young people are feeling insecure about their identity and looks; this is often fueled by image magazines. It is not just the size of the models but also the unrealistic lifestyles. Some parents often work long hours, so that harsh sanctions are not imposed upon the family but this can also leave the young people vulnerable, and susceptible.

People's needs in society are not being acknowledged, or disregarded. Often when a person have their needs met they don't consider those of other people. Some policies makers can inflict harm upon others, due to their own lack of experience and knowledge in this area. There is also little awareness of international laws, and criminal laws so decisions are often made on a whim without any form of legal consideration, a failure to implement laws in the decision making policy. The "me me me" mindset has to look at what it is creating; I find the allegory of -the long handled spoon- moral, very apt.

There have been a lot of members within society's damage someone's life and on their other hand give to charity, these double standards are sending out mixed messages.

I have noticed an attack on poor vulnerable people. It is easy to kick a person when they are down but it takes a real hero or a Good Samaritan to help. It also appears that it has become a personal war between the political parties, but they are all forgetting they are meant to support the people and not attack them with abusive policies which often breach the law.

Mental health issue is at an all time high, why are so many people suffering? There is a complete lack of transparency or fudged data to protect those who are filling in the policy, whilst real vulnerable people suffer. Why would these decision makers care? We are living in a society where care seems to be invisible.

We in the UK have a benefit system, which attacks personal independence payment (pip) claimants; the assessors often says the claimants good regardless of doctors medical evidence or psychologist reports or other evidence to say the claimants are fit to work and thus not entitled, when pip is also for the working person. This support is meant to focus on disability; however people still ironically have their disability regardless of what an assessor says. This benefit discriminates and breaches international human rights laws. For those who have had a heart attack, or learning needs, mental health and the doctor lays them off work- the pip assessor says they are fit to work and the needs a not high enough for help. The UK benefits system is not a safety net, and it's discriminatory in many aspects. This system is murderous at times and statistics reveal this too. The benefit system needs to change and to be brought into to accordance with human rights laws. Supporting all disabilities and allowing all claimants enough to be able to afford food and have a safe place to live. Due to the expensive housing, people spend most of their money on rent, single parents are caught in an unfair trap with high rents and high childcare which actually often puts them into debt, the toll upon a child also leaves many vulnerable.

As I wrote this book I found so many people are suffering with mental health and cannot access help, so I hope some of this information will hopefully be of benefit to you. The information on the brain and foods will help readers to have more awareness and control, understanding on what is happening to your brain when you get stressed or anxious and what you can do to help yourself.

My own personal awareness of my research was: liberating. The truth was somewhat painful at times. I went through a lot of unstable hours whilst processing my thoughts and feelings associated with the abuses. However after processing the information I found acceptance and forgiveness.

Now, I am not particularly religious, and I am not saying your religion is better or worse than what I believe, but I do believe in Jesus. My faith kept me going, also my new faith made me strong where I could walk away from people so that I could try to discern between who is toxic and who is supportive. I pressed into God many times and the answers weren't always what I was expecting. Sometimes you just need to push on the door a little harder but you also need to learn, if it doesn't open then it's not meant to.

People's aspirations are important. Every person is important. We all need to build each other up and not tear each other down.

The best advice, is – Be kind to yourself.

Breakthroughs

The idea of breakthroughs is so that the trauma has either no effect, or it has a lesser effect on you, so you have a better quality of life. Once you have a breakthrough, you can feel completely different about yourself, and you may notice that the heavy burden has lifted. You may feel happier or just able to do things you haven't been able to do for a long time due to flashbacks, anxiety, and depression etc. There are therapies and methods that can be supportive.

I don't see many saints around daily, however I do see many people just trying to get on with their life the best they can. Some make good choices and some make bad choices and live with the consequences. When people make bad choices then they need to forgive themselves and try not to repeat it. People shouldn't beat themselves up because things didn't turn out the way they had hoped.

Often our motive is stemmed by our desire; Money, clothes, holidays, control, creating something, loyalty etc. We all want different things. People with low self esteem or confidence often don't know what they want and look at other people they admire and imitate those qualities. When people have self esteem they don't need to look to others for reassurance, or to imitate because of being comfortable with their own visions, or are in a comfortable position.

Forgive- atone, to make it right as best you can, or make amends. If someone has abused you then, let go and forgive the person, however this doesn't mean you should allow them to repeat abuse. Forgiving yourself is especially important and particularly if you have been a victim/survivor or a soldier. A survivor may have started out with a good intention, but the perpetrator could exploit the victim's loyalty or love against them. This is an impossible dichotomy, so release responsibly, as any ethical decision had been removed.

Cogitation is rationalizing the issue that can't be solved by any action, i.e, if you shot someone, or a trafficker died, or the child stole a loaf of bread to be able to eat. The victim or serviceman have often conducted these actions, and finds, that past action now frequently torments them, and drives them to despair. It is also known as; when the devil has got a stronghold, which can be mentally destructive. Predators rarely take responsibility, as they pass it over to their mules, worker or victims that had carried out the task. The master minds often walk free allowing victims to take the fall and live in fear.

So many children, people and platoons etc, are often carrying out orders. Often, if the objective is of a questionable nature then a person following out an order is often unprepared for the psychological impact, i.e trafficked people, war veterans, and teenagers led astray, and convicts are often victims of exploitation. It is a capital offence if you break an oath as a service person, and many child soldiers who signed up at a young impressionable age often find they ruminate and regret their actions when they become older, as do trafficked people, or convicts, which have often been lured into a situation. Often the decisions people make at a younger age are naïve and lead them to suffer due to a sugar coated promise. Child solders also suffer from Stockholm syndrome. Children and younger people can often cut themselves off from their past (disassociation) to form a new identity which is more appropriate to their current situation, and often imitate the behavior of their leaders.

Whatever happened in the past is in the past, however, It is often persistent negative memories that are an issue; this can be supported and processed with several techniques. Negative attachment needs to be relinquished so that the wounds can heal.

There are many techniques, laws, greater awareness of behavior, faith, exercise, space for processing your thoughts will support you towards your breakthrough.

With my own breakthroughs I implemented several techniques and pressed into God, with adopting many aspects of the New Testament. My mental obstructions dissipated leaving me with a greater awareness and more freedoms. Prior to my traumas and at several times throughout my life I was incredibly vulnerable and highly susceptible to being led astray, which is what happened. As I reflected on my past, it is clearly obvious I faced several perilous situations, where I was unprepared and ill equipped to deal with my experiences/traumas. Now I have moved on and forgiven, I am happy to talk about these issues which many consider taboo to bring greater awareness and to support others.

Faith

I actually personally find this very important. This is a personal belief system. Now faith is confidence in what we hope for and assurance about what we do not see, Hebrew 11:1. Sometimes when a person has their back against the wall, (figure of speech) then often all they have is their faith, or they find their faith. Faith often keeps the mind strong whereas without faith a person could be more susceptible to giving up, or low mood. This would indicate that mankind has always had a need to believe in something greater than themselves, i.e faith or a greater belief system.

There are plenty of different places of worship and prayer around the world; some are more gospel, some traditional. It is a personal choice of what you like. For me personally, I like the churches in the USA. They pull me in (metaphorically). I love listening to the Word, and it makes me feel lighter. The power of the word can also provide answers and hope, where normally there would be little. However so many people only turn to God when they are in need of solace and not daily for gratitude.

There is so much wisdom in the Bible for example: different patterns of behaviors, thinking, a timeline of historical events, Different characters, (Prostitute, Carpenters, Kings, Prophets etc) how these character interacted with other people. How they would rule/ control, How God influenced their lives, future events, etc.

The timeline of the Old Testament does prophesizes events. The New Testament has confirms many prophesies, and are still being fulfilled today. Jesus used parables to express complex concepts in the form of timeless simple stories which could communicate with the masses.

Jesus often spoke of the heart. Luke 16:15 :and he said to them- "you, are those who justify yourself- in the sight of men, but God knows your hearts: for that which is highly esteemed among men, is detestable in the sight of God.

Progression of thinking/ behavior

Timeline of marriage in the bible: In Deuteronomy 24:1 (Old Testament) it says that a husband can divorce his wife if he found something objectionable about her. However a woman could not initiate a divorce. However Jesus (New Testament) Mathew 19: 8, Jesus replied, "Moses permitted you to divorce your wives because your hearts were hard. But it was not this way from the beginning. In modern life there are many people who marry, divorce, with woman instigating divorce also. This can identify changes in behavior, and within interpersonal relationships. There are many new factors in today's society that were not considered previously like: work, geographical location of a spouse. Today we experience more changing dynamics; however faith has become all the more important.

Discrimination:

In the Old Testament Abraham suggests- there are two types of people in this world.

1. His opponents, show themselves to be the children of the slave woman, who was sent out to the wilderness

2. The children of the Promised Land.

This would have caused many years of division between these people. After 400 years of silence, from God, (Isaiah 29:10). John the Baptist came from the Judean wilderness – and began to cry out. "Repent, for the kingdom of heaven is near" (Matthew 3:2). This man was without airs and graces, and he was also known for being somewhat blunt with people in the crowd, he was unknown until the day he was revealed to Israel. John did not know Jesus was the promised Messiah until he baptized him. John 1:33.

John the Baptist was spreading God's word, who came out from the wilderness and would have conflicted with Abrahams children, of the Promised Land. John said to them: Don't just say to each other, "we are safe, for we are descendants of Abraham"! That means nothing.. For I tell you, God can create children of Abraham, from these very stones.. Mathew 3:9-

My point is or moral behind this is:

1. Those who don't feel they fit in, due to being discriminated against, should know that God works above and beyond human comprehension. God can change things in a blink of an eye.

2. This is an example of a psychological change in the mind set of the people. Many people repented, which would release all the self blame, guilt, and wrong doing, and even toxic thoughts which would have supported the people in the renewing of the mind.

Jesus' teachings supported this transformation with powerful messages and parables, which is likened to the book of proverbs, in the Old

Testament, as well as perform miracles. This renewed many people's faith in which before they had none.

Recently, I listened to a pastor talking about planting ourselves. He used the forest analogy with a storm: A tree generally has roots that go deep into the earth, and hold firm in a storm. Redwood trees only go down two meters. Even though the trees are mighty tall, the roots reach out to other redwood trees, and bind together supporting each other, allowing them to weather a storm. They need each other's support, just like we need the support of positive people around us to help hold us up in the storm. I hope my book supports all of you. Be strong in who you are.

Other Things I Implemented

Metaphors:

In Japan if an object is broken, it's mended with glue, and then the cracks are painted gold. This shows that where an object has been damaged, it is restored stronger and more beautiful than it was before. This metaphor shows that each human can be strengthened and can become more beautiful. So do not be afraid to show your scars. The wisdom is that all the scars and breaks are beautiful. In your journals, you will discover your own wisdom and beauty. Jesus heals the broken-hearted.

Simile:

Over the years I had collected lots of things, i.e, clothes, furnishings, music equipment, tools that I never use etc, and just collecting dust. My house is very small and I complained about the lack of space so I decided to just clear out the lot. I did have to be ruthless at times because it was tempting just to hold on to the stuff. So I went through my house from cupboard to cupboard and threw everything out that I never used or probably will never use in the future. Some of the items I had sold went to people who were looking for what I was selling, so my junk became their treasure. My house became fresh and more spacious. I made more space for exercising and felt better by not holding on to all that past junk. I assimilated this to my mind; I needed to clear out all the junk that was no longer serving me. It felt great to get rid of it. De-junking the mind of negativity is like spring cleaning the house and it's liberating.

Diet:

Generally, I am pretty healthy with my food, and I cook fresh food without additives. However, I increased my fruit consumption so I'd have more natural vitamins.

Calm Area:

Creating a calm safe place supports personal control.

Affirmations:

These are often modern positive quotes made by different people to help lift a negative mindset. Here are my favorite affirmations:

- 'Although the world is full of suffering, it is also full of overcoming of it' (Helen Keller).
- 'I know God will not give me anything I cannot handle. I just wish he didn't trust me as much' (Mother Teresa).
- 'The flower doesn't think of competing with the flower next to it . . . it just blooms' (Zen Shin)
- 'Sometimes the people around you won't understand your journey; they don't need to, as it's not for them.'

Getting through It

A Healing journey is a self reflecting process which a person can use after a trauma or an unpleasant event, so that a person can understand how that event has affected them. This can highlight changes in behavior often associated to the cause. It will also identify what your coping strategy is and if it is healthy or not. This awareness also empowers a person to be able to change bad habits.

Find a safe place and remove all distractions. Relax and take deep breaths. As you breathe you can focus on different parts of the body. If the body is not relaxed it will remain more rigid.

There are exercises to shake out stress, any physical tension in your body by shaking your body through a trauma release exercise (TRE).

When you body is more relaxed and you feel safe, then you can look at starting your journal. There are several thoughts and feelings that you will need to process and this will need to be written down (see journal). You must accept what you have experienced and forgive yourself for holding on to any pain, guilt or shame.

If you're not ready to write down your thoughts and feelings then use this time to express yourself through arts and creative mediums.

Any form of expression, or writing will help you to offload the negativity, and will help mentally and physically.

There are also several types of workshops for well being and there are one to one based therapists who can implement different techniques. Not exclusive list

- Setting boundaries
- Confidence
- Stress Reduction

Your journal is private, and you do not need to discuss any detail with anyone. Some memories can be challenging, and this may bring up painful thoughts that were not fully processed. Try to focus on your present surroundings and feel the texture, and smell the air, this can help you to focus on where you are, and help you to recognize that you're in a safe environment. This is about being aware of your current environment, it detracts your mind from the past toxic trauma, to you present safe place. However if there are areas causing you to become emotionally uneasy then it is advisable to consult a therapist. As you process past toxic thoughts and emotions then they should dissipate and have a lesser hold over you.

Go easy on yourself.

Know that all problems are like clouds. They all pass eventually.

Proverbs 3:5-6 Trust the lord with all your heart and lean not on your own understanding, in all your ways submit to him and he will make your paths straight.

Journaling Exercises

The objective of both journals is to clearly see the events and behaviors which correlate to the trauma. This can help to you to identify a lot, and gives you greater understanding and control over toxic thoughts and behavior. You will not have to re-live the trauma, however you will process your thoughts and feelings in association to the event.

Journal 1: Events. Write your life events down on a timeline, stating the year and month. This way you can identify what happened in what year (i.e. holiday to Africa in 1999, school in 1986–1987 and netball team, went on school trip, etc.).

This will be factual information only. If the timeline has a painful experience then just write in the word "sensitive" without having to elaborate on the type of abuse. The timeline is a line of all major events in your life.

6	school	
7	sensitive	
8	sensitive	
9	school - holidays	
10	school-holidays	
11	school-holidays	
12	school holidays	
13	school - holidays	
15	sensitive	
16	sensitive	
17	moved to bedsit, new job	
18	met boyfriend	
19	sensitive	working
20	sensitive	working

The second journal is about how the event or trauma made you feel, and how it makes you behave etc.

What's the difference between Emotions and Feelings?

- Emotions: Are often expressed through the body and facial expression, and can be visually observed, i.e, Fear, Disgust, Happiness, Sadness, and Contempt etc. Emotions create a movement, or action. People give rise to their emotions as it is a reaction to a stimulus. It's instinctive and a physical reaction to a threat or stimulus. Emotions are a reaction that comes from a surge of hormones, which has been processed in the Amygdala. The amygdala is involved in fear memories. When a person has a nightmare or flashbacks in their sleep, it is a memory stored in the Amygdala; this combined with an emotional response in their sleep can leave the survivor disorientated and reliving this experience.

- Emotional blocks: Are often absent physical reactions, this may-be because they are suppressed and just not felt. Some people will not always express themselves emotionally and can internalize the pain; this can contribute to mental health/ wellbeing issues. Arts are a very supportive method to express how they feel.
- Feelings: Are often internalized and processed by the mind, and not often seen. Feelings are often thought provoked. Anxiety is a feeling, and can be stimulated by a person's thought. Some anxious people may exhibit fidgety habits related to this internal feeling. Confidence is also an internal feeling and not a behavior. A positive feeling can be a motivating factor. A negative feeling can render motivation.

Journal 2: Emotions and feelings:

Use another book and correlate the dates and your feelings, how do you feel about these traumas or events? Do not write what happened but only how you felt and how it makes you feel now. This book is often more creative with words, thoughts, feelings, how you behave, and scribbles. You can use emoji if this is too painful to talk about. If the pain is so bad then circle this! This maybe one area you want to address with a professional therapist.

Use different colors also to highlight different feelings and emotions. This will highlight for your journal

- Emotional: Anger(red) Sad(Brown)- Happy(yellow), Love (pink), (Impartial emotions) etc
- Feelings: Anxiety(grey)- Fear(black)- joy(blue) Depressed(orange) (Impartial feelings) etc

As you go through your second book, it may start to look very colorful. You can establish triggers and your reactions. This is all in the past.

How does this make you feel? What makes you feel this? How do you react? The list is not exclusive. Give these all a color to how it affects you i.e Loud noise (red)

- Upset
- Loud noise
- Sad
- Guilty
- Bored
- Hungry
- Happy
- Confident
- Listen to music
- Go on holiday
- Fear
- Scared
- Love
- Excited
- Calm
- Disgusted
- Comedy
- A Childs playground
- An garden
- Cars
- Hostage
- A couple arguing
- Gun
- Add your own...

What makes you feel this? As in the questions above are often your triggers. i.e, a Comedy is the trigger to joy(blue)or A gun could be a trigger to fear(black)

How do you react to fear? Reactions: Fight- Flight- Freeze

How do you react to Anxiety? etc

Awareness:

Thoughts and feelings is how we interpret what's happened externally to us. This is often projected out in the way we behave, but not always. If a person bought you a jumper then that may create pleasant feelings. Your reaction might be possibly to try it on. (Motivating)

Story reaction

If a person came up to you, shouting and swearing at you, then what is your reaction? Is it frozen with fear, to hit him, or run away?

Now if I told you that man had tourettes syndrome, which is neurological disorder and he is compelled to swear due to the disorder, would you re-think about how you would react now?

So by changing the story of the fear, you can see it differently. Instead of fear you may feel pity and compassion for the person who is afflicted with tourettes.

Now, you can identify that your reaction to the trigger has changed. Once the fear is removed then the reaction will be less evoking.

After a trigger has gone off, and you either took off froze or punched a few people and you need to calm down then what do you do? Look at your triggers on here and think about what you have done. These are your coping strategies. Write all of yours down. When you see yourself doing any of these then look around to see if a trigger has gone off and what has made you do this? Often the trigger could be indirectly associated to the trauma and it hasn't been identified until you look at this. This has become your habit to deal with your stress. Reflect back over your journal and view this in third hand, like you are reading somebody else's story. (Desensitizing)

You can't changed your innate reactions to a stimulus, but you can change the story behind the trigger, which often belongs in the past, by creating a new story, I.e, this will desensitize and lessen any impact. A therapist can support a survivor with these exercises, NLP, Re-framing, psych-k.

Habits; are created by repetition. We can also change our habits but we need to recognize them in order to change this.

Some abused or traumatized victims often we deny certain feelings and emotions, and denial can be a habit. Being aware of feelings and emotions give a person more control.

Coping strategies: are also habits that have been formed to help a person calm down. You can change these if you find it is not supportive to your health and wellbeing.

Look for:

- Repeating behavior patterns
- Repeating habits
- Repeating thoughts or feelings
- Repeated gaps in thinking or behavior

Flashbacks: can emotionally heighten a person's awareness and cause insurmountable stress; however, if you understand this stress is due to a past event, and then you can immediately lower the stress levels. One way of doing this is to identify how you react to flashbacks and triggers, what is your coping strategy (The exercise earlier). Once you can identify this, then you can gain control quicker.

Learning styles:

- Audio: Church, Prayer groups, Hemi sync audios frequencies to create new positive neuro pathways; this is more for audio learners which creates new thinking into positive thoughts. NLP. Music

- Visual: Journal: Bible, affirmations, Art, Color therapy, observe your own behavior, Observe habits, reframing by NLP

- Kinesthetic: Create new habits by identifying what you want to change, by changing the habit creates new neuro-pathways. NLP:, Tapping, PSYCH-K, Exercise, Cognitive therapy groups – is about awareness and how your external world affects your feelings and emotions. This will often be observed in behavior.
- Change thinking into positive thoughts; creates new neuro pathways. These positive thoughts start to diminish the negative thoughts; this allows a person more mental freedoms and reduces painful memories. It is not a quick process and the traumatic memory of the event will always be there but what can change is lessening the impact or negativity it has on your-selves by new neuro pathways.. Greater understanding, Positive steps:

Reading daily affirmations, being grateful, create positive thinking; Prayer groups and some churches also have immense support and can spiritually lift you up. Try a new hobby. if you aim to high to fast it will often be counterproductive and disappointing, smaller steps are often more constructive in development, so go easy on yourself as you change your lifestyle.

If you notice you've regressed back to old habits or stress, then go back to your notes. Make sure you write down what is helping you so you can always pull up these notes if you need to. Remember to treat yourself with love. With any therapy and healing, the objective is that you come out feeling more positive. There will be times that you may feel overwhelmed with emotion, but this is also normal when you are reflecting back. Sometimes it can be very painful when you look back and see what you have been through. There is no rush, and this may take years. But remember, you are now safe. 'One day I will wipe away every tear from your eyes.

And I will take away all the pain you have suffered on this earth' (Revelation 21:3–4). 'I am also the Father who comforts you in all your troubles

What to Expect after

Before your therapy, you may have experienced panic attacks and anxiety in response to a past trauma, being a trigger; however, these attacks should be lessening or fading away. If an unexpected trigger does happen, you aware of what is happening to you, physically and mentally.

You have learnt to identify how the external world affects the way you feel and often behave. You would have been able to identify different techniques that may support you in your development.

Learnt to embrace change, and start to look at healthier ways of living. Learn to be kind to yourself, and reflect back on your notes if you regress back to old habits. You may feel more confident, and the walls you once had will start to fall away, releasing a newer way of life. Keep expanding your horizons, and keep reflecting on the personal distance you have travelled. This will increase your self-esteem, and you should feel really proud of yourself. Try new things, and spontaneity.

When you reflect back over the journal, remember, your future can be very different to your past. Your past doesn't define you. Let go of any blame that is holding you back from living in the current moment.

As much as we can learn to move on, we also need to address prevention.

When a person is vulnerable they need to be able to access support. Some vulnerabilities lead people into a perilous situation, which can traumatize people for many years. We need to be pro active with international human rights and bring policies into line to protect those who are vulnerable. Empower yourself and empower others.

'You are fearfully and wonderfully made' (Psalm 139:14).

Love Yourself

'You were not a mistake for all your days are written in my book' (Psalm 139:15–16).

Why is it so difficult to love ourselves?

Often after a traumatic experience or limiting beliefs there are a host of negative emotions and feelings. Any blame, guilt, self hate, loathing can chip away at self worth or respect. If we allow our external world (other opinions) to dictate how we are, then we can't build up self –esteem and a healthy self love, respect for ourselves.

Ultimately, we believe we don't deserve- we accept only what we think we deserve as that has been either conditioned externally or internally by our own low worth. We stay in our limited comfort zone. Low self worth can make us accept what we are only comfortable with and not our actual worth.

Having insecurities can make a person either more controlling or timid. Often the person rejects someone or something amazing, because it makes them feel uncomfortable and undeserving. You should never feel embarrassed or uncomfortable over a compliment. You should never feel like you're not good enough. If God loves us unconditionally then why don't you love yourself unconditionally?

When you love yourself, you're giving by nature; you have expansive energy. When you love yourself, you grow more than you ever realize is possible, and there are no restraints to personal development.

When you have impaired self-esteem, then you are looking externally for approval; however, self-esteem comes from your internal being. Know you are worthy.

Don't criticize yourself or your situation. Understand that life can change and you just have to be kind to yourself as you are waiting for that to happen. Try to construct some activities that you enjoy. Take time out for you to make or do something positive. When you start to love yourself, you will start to gravitate more to what makes you happy and less to what makes you unhappy. You are worth it.

Know you are accepted and loved by God always.

What Is Self-Love?

Self-love is about acceptance and valuing yourself. Accept that life does throw obstacles in your path, and learn to overcome them and enjoy the challenge. It is important to respect yourself and not to let others control your situation; this is often a challenge for victims. Your voice is just as important as any other person's. Be kind to yourself and treat yourself well. Let go of past issues so you can enjoy life. Rebuilding your life is not instantaneous or a one-time action and neither is self-love. This requires continuous respect and kindness to your-self.

Self-love is not about being egotistical or having abundant possessions; it is about being and feeling worthy. It is showing compassion to yourself and others around you and not judging yourself or others. It is not being harsh to yourself or mentally beating yourself; it's about learning to be yourself with all your flaws and having fun being you. It is about accepting yourself just as you are and still enjoying life—your life. Look in the mirror daily, and say something positive about yourself. When you are your true self, you shine. Self-love is about inner beauty and confidence. It's not about how magazines or anyone else tells you how to be. Self-love is something you feel.

'When you are broken hearted I am close to you' (Psalm 34:18).

CHAPTER 11

Final Thoughts

The body and mind are intrinsically joined, and in order to maintain good health, then both must be respected. Abuse can contribute to poor mental and physical health as well as long-term suffering. This book has identified many types of abuses and harmful effects on victims and survivors.

It may take many years before a person can feel safe enough to be able to start the healing process. Abuses can lead to long-term psychological insecurity, self-doubt, guilt, and a whole host of negativities. When I started my healing process, I became aware of how vulnerable I had been. As the healing started to unfold, I felt more scared that there had been so few safety nets in place and how hard it was to access help. So I felt it was important to create a wider awareness and provide helpline numbers, which are available throughout this book. All victims and survivors deserve to feel safe and have access to safety and support, where they can begin to heal. We need to build each other up and not tear each other down. No one should be left to suffer.

Anyone can be a victim through no fault of their own but through circumstances. I learned that the guilt and shame I felt all those years ago belonged to the perpetrators and not myself. I will not take ownership for their evils. I hope that my breakthrough can offer support to my readers. The information contained herein cannot replace the services of trained professionals, but it is my own experiences and my breakthrough. It took many years before my breakthrough due to me not being in a safe environment or the timing not being right. I did have to dedicate time for this healing process and eliminate distractions which weren't possible previously. For me, my arduous healing journey changed my life. It gave me closure, and I learned to forgive and move on.

People need a voice; many people are trapped in perilous situations due to their circumstances. Some victims have fewer life chances, and there is no end to the abuse. Many abuses have become the norm for them that they are unaware they are being abused. This damaging existence is ruining communities, and the solution is for us to listen to the people at the deep roots and offer support.

Most victims will never report abuse due to the pain and humiliation they had experienced. Abuse survivors often feel exposed again through regurgitating up thoughts and feelings, so it is easier to stay quiet. There needs to be more compassion and understanding towards victims in court. Jail doesn't solve bad behavior or change abusive people, as they continue time and time again. Laws were once created by people to create fairness in society for all common persons; however, there is now a disparity between who can afford legal representation and who can't, which in itself isn't fair. So by definition of fair and the symbol of justice, the scales are somewhat unbalanced.

The crown that I won is a symbol of victory. I triumphed over all the abusers who stole my confidence, my self-esteem, and my self-worth and who kept tearing me down. Over the years, I felt so negative about myself and ashamed of my body. With the kind words of one person, I learned to see myself differently, and I learned how to build my confidence. Without those kind words, I may not be where I am today. Without my relationship with God, I may not feel whole, and I may have continued to carry on feeling needy. I am thankful that I have learned to build my life after my traumas and that there is light at the end of the tunnel.

I am thankful I persevered through the different therapies and prayers when I reached rock bottom. My life has not just improved; it surpassed any of my expectations. I never would have thought I would be doing beauty pageants in my forties—and winning them nonetheless! I never thought I would be in feature films or have lead roles in my forties. I had so many people telling me in my thirties that it was past my time now and that I'd missed the boat, and I heard so many negatives. But let me tell you this: what they said was nothing but a bunch of lies. God can turn our lives around, through Jesus and it may never be the same again.

The crown symbolizes for me victory over my oppressors. The beauty crown is not just my victory but a victory for all the survivors of abuse. I dedicate this crown to you, which can be seen on the back cover.

You are all beautiful. Don't let anyone tell you different. They tried to break us, but instead we will rise victoriously.

BIBLIOGRAPHY

Alexander Stille *http://www.newyorker.com/news/news-desk/what-pope-benedict-knew-about-abuse-in-the-catholic-church 02/01/2017*.14 Jan 2016 -

ALEXANDER SMITHU.N. Report: Vatican Policies Allowed Priests To Rape Children(FEB 5 2014)

Amelia Gentleman- People getting a criminal record for not being able to pay for a TV licence.- the Guardian(Wed 24 Sep 2014)

Angela Smith -(Penistone and Stocksbridge) (Lab)Domestic Abuse Victims in Family Law Courts15 September 2016.

Boyle, Danny, 'Harriot Harmon sex in return for higher degree in politics-, The telegraph-(27/01/2017).

David D. Kirkpatrick, Danny Hakim and James Glanz-Why Grenfell Tower Burned: Regulators Put Cost Before Safety 24/June/2017

Davidson, Tom, 'Paedophile Ex-Cop Gordon Anlesea Dies in Prison Hospital', (16/12/2016).

Eleanor Tucker The Telegraph by (13 April 2014).

Edward J. Carnot 1656 - Is Your Parent in Good Hands? Protecting Your Aging Parent from Financial Abuse and Neglect, (Capital Cares) (2003-11-13).

Kate West- Liverpool Royal School for the Blind headmistress 'abused children' (BBC news 9 January 2017)

'Harriet Harman Talks to Andrew Marr', BBC (29 January 2017). University Lecture offered her sex in order to gain higher grades

Hilary Osborne- Poverty premium: why it costs so much more to be poor – THE Guardian-(Tue 10 Nov 2015)

J. Douglas Bremner, The traumatic effects on the brain https://www.ncbi.nlm.nih.gov/pmc/articles/PMC3181836/ (2006 Dec; 8)

Lanville, Sandra, https://www.theguardian.com/society/2016/dec/22/revealed-how-family-courts-allow-abusers-to-torment-their-victims

Lisa A. Goodman - American Journal of Orthopsychiatry financial cuts leading to more suicides(1991) 2015/16

Lloys, Sian, Gordon Anglesea Paedophile Ex-Police Boss Gets 12 Years, BBC News(04/11/2016).

McDermott, Mat, 'Monsanto Shifts All Liabilities for Damages Caused by Its GM Crop to Farmers', 05/11/2016 www.treehugger.com, 02/25/2011.

Nicola Harley - Jimmy Savile caught on camera groping a girl in front of her mother - 2 - www.telegraph.co.uk/news/2016/ OCTOBER 2016-

Nigel Ward. https://www.whatdotheyknow.com/user/nigel ward- Whitby Schools Safeguarding from The Examiner 9 February 2016

Roubicek, Joe, Financial Abuse of the Elderly: A Detective's Case Files of Exploitation Crimes (2008).

Rowan Moore Britain's housing crisis is a human disaster. Here are 10 ways to solve it- The Guardian (March 2015)

Sky news - Football abuse victim Andy Woodward demands full investigation at Crewe-football clubs https://news.sky.com/story/football-abuse-victim-andy-woodward-demands-full-investigation-at-crewe-10673003Saturday 26 November 2016

Unknown author - Child abuse whistle-blowing helpline launched by NSPCC and Home Officehttp://www.bbc.co.uk/news/uk-35566253 (13 February 2016)

Unknown author- Historical child abuse: Key investigations- https://www.bbc.co.uk/news/uk-28194271- 1 December 2015

Unknown author-bbc- Ex-Ashdown House School teacher jailed for pupil sex offences 24 March 2017

INDEX

Lightning Source UK Ltd.
Milton Keynes UK
UKHW040640070919
349308UK00001B/36/P